# Diana Love Story (PT. 1 + PT.2)

## I began dating the second smartest girl in the community.

## Tina Scott

In my senior year of high school, March 1979, I began dating the class brain. She wasn't anyone I asked out, and she wasn't the sort of person I'd normally ask out. Diana had long brown Hair and large plastic frames, and she looked a little mousy. Under layers of clothing, she seemed to have a decent body, but it was difficult to say for sure. She was also the shy one and didn't have many contacts. So no one knew anything about her except that she was vying with Elizabeth Chen for the title of class valedictorian. The third position was too far away to make a difference.

I wasn't exactly a class stud. I did okay; I'd gotten laid by a couple of different ladies, but none of them was my true love. I dated a few girls but never got involved with any of them. I had dark brown hair and eyebrows, a 70s beard, and thicker Hair than was now considered natural. Stocky but not chubby, I was on the wrestling squad and enjoyed playing softball and football with my parents. I had good grades and SAT scores, but I wasn't a fool. In March of my senior year, 1979, I decided to attend Binghamton, a difficult school in the State of New York college system. I thought I was up to the task.

I was walking down the hall with my buddy Mike (sorry, I'm Jon) after classes one day in mid-March on our way to the Student Government office (he was class VP, and I was a 'delegate') when we saw Diana sitting on the floor against the tiled wall, red in the face, a portrait of frustration. Here, I didn't KNOW Diana, but I did know her. We went to Hebrew school together from eight to thirteen and then to public school beginning in seventh grade. So we had known each other for a long time, but it was more like a passing relationship than anything else. I don't recall ever having a chat with her.

I said this as I passed by. "Diana, how are you doing? Is there anything I can do for you?" Mike stared at me with a 'what the heck' smile on his face, and I just shrugged.

"No, you can't help," she replied, "but thank you for asking," I told Mike that he could keep driving and that I'd catch up with him later.

I sat a few inches away from her on the tiles, set my books down, and said, "If you like, you should chat about whatever is troubling you. I'm a decent listener."

"Do you genuinely worry, Jon? We've been friends for almost a decade, and you've never spoken five things to me at once. Why is this happening now?"

"Diana, if you want me to accompany you, I can do so. I just figured you seemed upset and in need of someone to speak to." I stood up and began walking towards the SG bed.

"Wait, Jon. I'm sorry; I should not have been so impolite. Could you please take a seat? I sincerely apologize." I sat down again after turning around.

"Diana, you are right. We've never spoken more than a couple of sentences to each other in all these years. But don't worry about it. If you like, you should tell me what's wrong. Alternatively, I will hold your company." Looking through her shades, she has lovely light blue eyes. Her cheekbones were prominent. At the very least, she was adorable and may have been much cuter with a little lipstick or a new haircut. It's everything. Maybe she just wanted something to make her happy.

"I have a few friends here, and none of them is very near. I have a near relative, but she lives in Chicago and many close buddies from years of going to the sleepaway lake, both as a camper and a counselor. When I go out, I meet up with some of them, but no one lives this close to me." She made a disappointed motion by blowing out her breath. "Elizabeth would be the valedictorian, according to what I've seen. Salutatorian, I get the booby prize. It's a big deal."

"I'm sorry, Diana. I can only imagine how dissatisfied you are. Consider things this way. About 300 of your classmates aspire to be in your shoes. At least, the majority of them will. I very certainly will."

"You wouldn't, will you? You have a lot of contacts and are well-liked. I'd give up my second position for any decent buddies here."

"Yes, but will you give up the first place?" With a grin, I said.

She returned my smile, the first genuine one I'd ever seen from her. "Most likely not. I'm a fierce competitor."

"Being successful is not a bad thing. When I wrestle, I'm like that. Still, unlike you, I'm just average at it. I have some wins and some losses. That's fine; it's not like it'll be a job decision. Binghamton University does not yet have a wrestling team."

"Are you heading to Binghamton? I'm the same way!" She said this with a pleasant surprise.

"What do you think? We'll each see at least one individual we meet. We will be each other's cheerleaders."

Diana's smile widened. It improved her look significantly. Her teeth were white and evenly spaced. When she grinned, her cheekbones were much more prominent. However, her Hair...

"Do you mind if I touch your Hair, Diana? It's all your Hair. I'm not starting over with you." She seemed suspicious, but she said okay, so I reached over and collected her Hair, pulling it back behind her. It revealed her complete profile, and the result was incredible. Then I asked her to remove her glasses, and when she did, my heart skipped a beat. Her eyes were stunning, and she looked much better with her mask less veiled. "Diana, do you have some mirror in your purse? You can look at what I see right now."

I let go of her Hair as she rummaged in her purse for a tiny mirror. Diana glanced in the mirror as I pushed her hair back again. It had to be the first time she saw herself like that because her eyes opened, as though she was taken aback by her presence. "Oh my goodness..." She shifted her gaze from side to side, not really, but enough to see herself in profile, then straight ahead. "Is it you? That's who I am."

"That's you," I said. "With a new hairstyle and maybe some contact lenses or a more modern pair of shades, you're stunning." But there was something else I found. I straightened her Hair and assisted her in putting her glasses back on. "You're also stunning in this outfit. I'd never seen it before. I didn't pay attention, and I'm sorry."

Diana wore a cynical expression on her lips. "I'm not this gorgeous, Jon. I'm aware that I'm a little plain."

"No way, no how. I'm not joking. "Talking to you like this, discovering you're a real human," I said, obviously amused, "you're lovely." If you change your appearance or not, you're quite pretty in any case. And I apologize if I made you feel like you have to improve to be beautiful. You are not required to. Feel at one with who you are."

Diana seemed as though she didn't know what to think of what I was doing. She had to have had little, or rather little, contact with men. "You're not playing games with me, are you, Jon? You wouldn't do anything like that to me, would you?"

"Scout's respect. I wasn't looking. That was a blunder. Do you want to go out this weekend? Saturday or Friday? It's you and me."

"Is it a date? Like going to the movies?"

"Yes, it's a date. But not a film. We don't know each other well enough to watch a movie quietly on our first date. Do you like Italian cuisine and beer?"

"I like it, but I prefer wine. And I'd like to accompany you. Friday evening."

"Done and done. If you want me to pick you up at 7 a.m.? I'm familiar with your street but not your address." She jotted it down for me, and we set a Friday date.

That happened on Tuesday. I had to go to my part-time job at a printing shop on Wednesdays and Thursdays from 3-6:30 and Saturdays from 11-5 to bring money in my wallet to go on a date the weekend and do some fun activities with colleagues. I enjoyed the position enough; the owner and his wife were good people, and the eight full-time employees were as well.

Friday afternoon, I showered and shaved before dressing in a nice pair of pants, a gold and red jumper, and brown shoes. Camilla, my 12-year-old niece, laughed as she saw me in front of the bathroom mirror, making sure my beard was even and slipping on cologne. "If you're going through all that hassle, she must be beautiful. Jon, what's her name? Please tell me! "She whimpered. My sister was adorable, bright, and sometimes a pain in the a$$. Thank goodness I adored her.

"Her name is Diana if you must remember," I said, focusing on the hairs above my lip. And, yeah, I think she's really attractive."

"She's really attractive, and she's going on a date with YOU?" Another chuckle. The boy had a thing for crushing my balls.

"That's right. If you're fortunate, a man will find you're attractive enough to ask you out when you're old enough. As in, when you're 65."

Camilla realized I was playing with her, so she walked off with a huge pout on her lips as though I had hurt her feelings. I didn't, and we were both aware of it. We each had our positions in the family. She was around four years out from the age at which our parents will allow her to date.

At 6:45 a.m., I put on a light sweater, took my keys to my '74 Ford, and said goodbye to my friends, promising them I'd be home by 1. I got in my vehicle, and by the time I arrived at Diana's house, it was almost 7 p.m. Right on cue.

I rang the doorbell, and a man who seemed to be her father replied. "Hello, Mr. Glazer? My name is Jon Grossman. I'm sure you're aware that I'm here to pick up Diana."

"Sure, come on in and take a seat. She isn't fully prepared yet. You already know how that goes, "With a chuckle, he said. I liked him from the start.

Two 14-year-old youth, clearly her twin brothers, were sitting on the floor in the living room watching television and paying little attention to me. Her mother emerged from the kitchen and approached me. "Hello, my name is Phyllis, and you met my uncle, Harold. Walt and Will are the two brats over there."

"Mom, we're not brats. We're just too busy, "one of them said "Too distracted to be courteous to a visitor?" Diana's whole family appealed to me. In several respects, they reminded me of my own. While we waited, her parents asked me a few questions, nothing too personal, just enough to know I had a part-time career, I was smart if not a genius like their daughter, and a few stuff about my parents. It was 7:15 p.m., and although I had been kept waiting by dates before, this was getting late, particularly for a casual date. Diana came downstairs a few minutes later, and I must say, she looked great. I always mean that. That's great. Her hair was swept back in a long ponytail, and she wore soft makeup to highlight her features. She didn't have any lenses, so she'd have to depend on contacts or have any difficulty seeing clearly. She was dressed in a dark green silk blouse and Calvin Klein pants, which were common with girls at the time thanks to Brooke Shields' sexy ad campaign. The jeans were a perfect match for her, as though they had been spray-painted over. I'm telling you, she looked fantastic. She would never have looked like that at college.

I got to my feet and said, "Diana, you look fantastic! Honestly. If you have connections on?"

"True. I've seen them for a long time but just carry them on special occasions." As a result, she regarded this as a rare moment. That's right; I did as well. I assisted her in putting on her hat, like keeping her ponytail back. We left after she promised her parents she wouldn't be late, whatever that meant. Diana grinned her appreciation when I opened the car door for her.

We spoke nervously on our way to a nearby Italian restaurant. From the outside, the establishment known as Marco's was unremarkable. It looked like a neighborhood bar at the bottom of a large suburban driveway, and it was, with around a dozen tables in the back in a poorly furnished space with checkered tablecloths. However, the food was delicious and reasonably priced—ideal for a high school student with a tight schedule.

Diana had never heard about it before and stared at me as though I were crazy before we went inside. She mistook me for a dive bar when I took her to a dive restaurant. We had to wait about 15 minutes for a table because it was busy, which is often a positive indication. I questioned whether she wanted white or red wine and then requested a carafe of the house red. I asked if she liked chicken, and when she said yes, I told her to disregard the menu because the chicken cacciatore was the best in town. Preparation took 45 minutes. She had faith in me, so I ordered it for both of us with ziti.

As we waited, we drank steadily enough that we didn't get more than a mild buzz, and we laughed and had a great time. We discovered a lot about each other. We also loved punk music from the 1960s and 1970s and despised disco. We both enjoyed reading books rather than those given to us at college. She wasn't a big fan of sports in general, but she did like baseball. She was a Mets fan, the Queens squad, but I was a Yankees fan. As we waited for our meals, we passed the time.

"Since I was a kid, I've never let someone order my food for me. "Then again, this is just the second date I've ever been on," she said openly. And the first one took place two years earlier." She kept my gaze; those beautiful blue eyes fixed on my brown eyes. Diana was not readily humiliated.

I assumed she didn't date much, but one date a couple of years ago surprised me. "If you don't mind me wondering, who was the date back then?"

"My family's mate. My family and his are good neighbors, and I've known Steven for almost my whole life. He's cool, but I'm not drawn to him. I went just to be able to say I'd been on a date. I've now seen two."

"Are you interested in me?" I inquired, both jokingly and enquiringly.

Her head leaned on the backs of both paws. "What are your thoughts? Is it just for a date that I'm out with you, or am I drawn to you?" She gave me a smile that, I hoped, gave away the secret.

"I believe you find me appealing. At the very least, I assume you do. Why else would you have accepted?"

"Maybe I appreciated how you spoke to me while I was down. Perhaps I find you amusing. And, to be frank, I think you're a handsome one. We do know you thought I was attractive. Why else would you have had to ask me out?" Diana maintained her gaze fixed on me. I could see she had a strong BS detector installed into her brain. My best bet was the facts. Almost always, it is.

"Well, you know, when I first saw you, I thought you were stunning, and I still do. When we first started chatting, I liked you as well. You have a wicked sense of humor. And, of course, you're very intelligent. That's what I look for in a lady. I'm sure a lot of guys find that overwhelming or off-putting. Just for me. I like a woman to be herself. And I'd rather be smart than ordinary. I despise stupid people in every way. So you have quite a few going for you. I'm not saying I'm God's gift to women."

When our food came, Diana was about to ask me another comment. Two large plates of a half chicken cut up, thinly breaded, and sauteed in a skillet before being baked with tomatoes, peas, and a rich tomato sauce served on a bed of ziti. I waited while she tried her food, and Diana, as predicted, loved it.

"Jon, this is awesome! Exceptionally tasty! Where did you discover this location?"

"A buddy of mine...you saw me walking with him the other day....brought me and another friend, Gil, here, and I've been coming ever since."

"Have you ever brought any ladies here?" Diana gave me a silly grin; it didn't matter to her.

"Yes, I do. Twice before. The food is excellent, it is reasonably priced, and it is limited enough that it is not too loud, allowing for simple conversation." We kept chatting as we ate, finding little tidbits about each other that weren't too serious. We ate slowly and didn't end until almost 9 p.m. I asked her if she wanted coffee and dessert after the plates were cleared.

"There would be no dessert. I couldn't eat much more! However, coffee will suffice. Caffeine-free."

I bought a decaf for her and tea for myself, and we stayed quiet for a few minutes after it was served. It was a pleasant silence; we were both having a pleasant evening. Diana approached me after a few moments. "Why did you ask me out, Jon? Honestly. You've seen me around for years, we've had some courses together, and you've ever seen me in the hallway. We just exchanged greetings. Why is this happening now?" As she sipped her drink, she cast a glance at me over the rim of her cup.

.

Once again, the reality was my best chance. In nearly any case, it almost always is. "Diana, it's basically what I said before. I considered you fascinating throughout our conversation. I already said that I dislike stupid people. Smart would not frighten me. And then, when we got together, I remembered how lovely you are, even with your glasses and Hair down. My heart skipped a beat when I pulled your hair back. I've never felt this way for a girl before. And, like you asked the other day, I'm not messing with you. Shame on me for not remembering you earlier. Shame on all the guys who have been ignoring you all this time."

Diana lowered her cup and stared down at the table. "As you may expect, I'm not used to being addressed in this manner. I'd never had any close girlfriends. A clever girl may also bully them. So reading all of your compliments makes me a bit uneasy. Maybe you're just saying sweet stuff so I can have sex with you as a conquest. Anything to be proud of."

"Hey, Diana, please look at me." She raised her head and stared me in the eyes. "I'm not trying to suggest why men don't do it because they do. Some men, just not everything. I don't think so. I've never had a significant relationship with a girl, and I can't choose the right one. I'll be completely truthful with you right now. I've had sex with a couple of different women. And based on what you've mentioned about one date with a man you weren't very feeling, I'm guessing you're a virgin. Tonight I'm having a great time with you. I'm going to request another appointment for you. Hopefully, this will happen again and again. And I assure you that nothing can happen between us before you are comfortable and want it to. There will be no squeezing or pulling. I guarantee it. After all, our date isn't done yet."

"That's a lot to process, Jon. I was hoping you'd invite me out again because I'm having a nice time tonight as well, although I have nothing to relate it to. But I don't think I need to compare. I'm having fun with a good man." She grinned broadly, and her expression ignited a little fire inside me. "Since you're so forthright with me, more forthright than I would have thought, I'll be forthright as well. Yes, I'm always a virgin. You know, I haven't exactly had a lot of chances. I'm not sure when it would improve. Tonight is not the night. "She added another grin to her face. "And I appreciate your assurance that there will be no pressure. I think you will stick to it. Who knows what will happen and where it will happen. You have mentioned that our date will not end tonight. What else were you planning?"

"Do you want to go see some live music? There are a few decent clubs nearby. Small establishments with live music most evenings. If you want to know more?"

"Sure thing. I've never been there before. Allow me to go to the lady's room."

Diana stood up, and I took control of the bill. As she came out, I helped her put on her coat again, which she loved, and we went to Poet's Corner. She had learned about it because it was just a few miles down from our high school. We were carded at the entrance and walked into the roar of rock and roll. It was still early, about 10, so it wasn't packed, and the music had been filmed, but it would shift by 11, but we were just in time. I asked Diana what she wanted to drink, and she replied, "What would YOU want to drink? This is all my fault."

"Okay, Diana. Come on. I invited you out. It's my pleasure."
"You paid for dinner. I'll pay for the drinks. I'd have to."
I'd never had a date, even once I'd been out with a couple of times, treat me to something. Diana's actions were admirable. She was not a self-centered individual in every sense. So I told her I'd have a glass of Beck's malt, and she rewarded me with a gin and tonic. We found a table that was not too close to the band, which was safer for our ears, and we drank while talking. Diana took my fingers in hers while I reached across the table and took her hand. Her hand was smooth and slim, very feminine, and her grip was welcoming. As the band started playing at about 11 p.m., the dance floor was packed with couples dancing to music by the Beatles, Bruce Springsteen, and others, and I asked her to join me.

"I'm sorry, Jon, but I don't know how to dance." Unless it's a baptism or a Bar Mitzvah." I joked, not at her, just to make her feel better.

"I'm not a huge fan of it myself. I'm sure you'll discover it's better than you thought." I extended my hand, and she reluctantly accompanied me to the floor. I was correct; it took a few attempts, but she eventually discovered a pattern for moving her feet and body, and we were dancing together in no time. Diana's petite body was quite lithe (she was 5'2" and slim with tiny breasts), and she loved herself naturally. She seemed unsure as slower music came on, and couples drifted closely together, keeping hands. I took a step closer to her and grasped her hips between my palms. She had her hands on my back, and we smiled at each other as we shuffled to the music. The mirror ball turned and reflected light all over her profile, making her eyes and whole face sparkle. Diana saw that other people wrapped their spouses' necks around theirs, so she stepped a bit closer so she could do the same to me. We had a big height gap (I'm 6'), and even with the three-inch shoes she was wearing, she had to lean her neck back to look into my eyes. I saw such amazing perfection in her, and seeing her body so similar to mine was exciting. My heart seemed to miss a beat every single beat. I wanted to kiss her, and I did so right on the dance floor.

Diana didn't shy down when I pecked her lips first. Instead, I noticed passion on her face and kissed her again, this time a light kiss that lingered; I could taste a hint of lipstick and got a good scent of some perfume she carried. Closed lips kisses were everything I went for in the bar, but they were fantastic. I would never have guessed she had never kissed a guy before.

I asked Diana if she wanted to quit after the song ended, and we all cheered the team. She agreed with a hesitant nod of her head. We gathered our jackets and her purse and proceeded to my vehicle. I drove a couple of blocks down the road to a quiet lane. It was now a little afternoon. I promised my parents I'd be home around one o'clock, so I didn't have a curfew. They were aware that I was on a date and that I might return home later. So if they didn't realize where I was, I had to be home by 2 p.m.

"Do you mind if we park and chat for a while?" I asked Diana. "Are you required to be home at a certain time?"

"We've got time. I will remain until around 2 p.m. And what you want to do is talk? "I was looking for more than just chat," she admitted, clearly flirting with me. I slipped across my big bench seat, and our lips touched again, except this time my tongue teased her lips, and they separated, allowing me in. We probed each other's throats, our tongues teasing each other back and forth, as our arms gripped each other tightly. I didn't want to persuade her because it might have contradicted what I had told her earlier about not pressing her. But after only 10 minutes, I had and tried to figure out where the line was. So I began running my hands across her back, and Diana did the same to

20

me. Then I aimed for her buttocks, and once again, there was no resistance and just reciprocity as she grabbed my cheeks with her tiny paws. She brushed my hand away when I wanted to touch her breasts, but she didn't interrupt our embrace. I understood where the line was now and valued it.

We hung out like that for more than an hour. Whenever we took a breather, we were both exhaling heavily with desire. I could see it in her expression, but it was our first date, and Diana wanted to take it slowly. The only thing was that I was as rigid as I had never been before, and my groin ached. But I didn't tell her that because it would put so much pressure on her, and I had vowed not to do so as excruciatingly painful as it was.

It was 1:30 by then, and I had to drive her home. I would have informed my parents later if I had learned we would have such a fun time. I had been out until 4 a.m., so I told them 1. As a result, two were pressing it.

We kissed again when we got to her place, not as aggressively this time, but with a strong desire for more. "Jon, I had the greatest night of my life last night. I'm hoping to hear from you over the break. I'd like to see you soon. Again and again. Not only at training, but that would be good as well. Only tell me one thing: are you going to forget me at school, or can you handle me as a friend?"

"I had intended to treat you as more than just an acquaintance. I don't mind if people realize we've been out and will continue to go out. I'd like you to meet some of my colleagues. Do you mind if we chat about this Sunday on the phone, Diana? I have to go to work tomorrow, and I need to relax." I didn't mention something of relaxation.

"I'm sorry, I forget you said you worked the next day." Have some rest. Please contact me on Sunday afternoon. "I'll be there." She had a lovely, warm smile on her face.

I kissed her again, gentle and loving. Even a smidgeononononononononononononononon Normally, I might have walked her to her house, but I couldn't get up right now. So I stood there watching her as she walked up the path to her door, waved goodnight, and drove off. I didn't have to worry about my parents because they were fast asleep. I changed into a pair of shorts, climbed into my bunk, took out my dick, and jerked off quickly, remembering how amazing Diana felt in my arms and on my tongue, and I came quickly. It wasn't because I wanted to make fun of myself. I decided to run out of there as soon as possible. As I arrived, I was soaked with sperm all over my hand and tummy. It solved my dilemma, but it would have been much superior if Diana had done it for me. I wanted to see you again.

XXXXXXXXXXXXXXXXXXXXXXXXXXXXXXXXXXXXXXXXXXXXX
XXXXXXXXXXXXXXXXXXXXXXXXXXXXXXXXXXXXXXXXXXXXX
XXXXXXXXXXXXXXXXXXXXXX

Saturday morning, I got up at 8 a.m., which was difficult given the conditions, and did my normal sets of sit-ups, push-ups, and other exercises to keep my body strong. Wrestling season had three more matches over the next two weeks, and I managed to win all three of them. I had eaten a lot the night before and wanted to lose more calories before going to work at 11 a.m. I jumped into the tub and went down to the kitchen to meet my friends. Camilla had gone out to a friend's house early. I had to leave for work in 40 minutes, leaving us only 20 minutes to meet.

"Good morning, Jon," mom said as she kissed the top of my head. "How was your date with.....Diana last night?"

"Yes, Diana, mum. It was fantastic. I very like her. We had a good time at dinner, then headed out for a beer and danced to live music." The rest wasn't their concern.

"Do you think you'll see her again?" my father asked.

"Oh, indeed. We've already discussed it. I informed her I'd contact her in the afternoon the next day. Work today, and a few of us are going to Richie's tonight. Nothing out of the ordinary, only freezing."

"Are there going to be girls there?" Dad inquired. Or is that the guys?"

"I'm not sure. Like I previously said, it is nothing extraordinary. "I'm just hanging out with my colleagues."

"I only think that if you like this kid, and there will be boys and girls, you can bring Diana."

"Dad, don't press it. I'm not sure what's going on there tonight, and as much as I like her, I don't want to hurry anything. Allow me to be gentle with her."

"That's what there is to it." I ate a small breakfast before heading to work. That night at Richie's, there were also ladies, mainly friends, and a handful of couples with some of my friends. It was laid-back, and a couple of joints were traded about. And I found myself worrying a lot about Diana. Someone had to call my attention at least twice as my mind drifted when I wondered of her. Oh my gosh, I was so into her. I was missing her.

And with the hits from the joints, thinking about it found it impossible to sleep that night. I tossed and turned for at least an hour, trying to decide how personal to Diana I needed to come. I hardly knew her as a human a week ago, and now, after only one (great) date, I wanted to get even closer to her. I could feel it in my bones: she was special. And I didn't have to be concerned with being so near and eventually being apart because we were both going to the same college in the fall.

As I called her the next day, I was still perplexed. I stated what was on my mind after sharing pleasantries and light talk. "I'm sorry, Diana. I'm feeling a bit guilty." Last night, I went to...well, not a dance, just a gathering of friends to hang out. And I find myself missing you, as though I was sorry I didn't invite you."

She let out a short chuckle. "Jon, we've just been on one date so far." "I grant you, it was a fantastic date," she said with a grin I could sense, "but it was just one date." So far, so nice. I wouldn't mind meeting your colleagues.

You owe nothing to me. But don't worry about it. But it's very kind of you to feel that way. "How did you spend your time at the 'gathering?'" She spoke softly.

"We just messed around, listened to music, and spread some marijuana around." The couples were given some anonymity. It's just not a huge deal."

"I've never experienced marijuana before. "I'm guessing you want it?"

"During the weekend. I never do it during the week, and I never do it while walking. Diana, would you like to go to the movies one weeknight? I'm assuming you don't still study."
"I suppose that's my status as a bookworm. It's infuriating. And, yes, I'd like to accompany you to the cinema that night. What night is it? I'll be able to make it tomorrow, Wednesday, or Thursday."
"So, how about tomorrow? If you want to see Hair?"

"That sounds amazing to me. It's a school night, so don't be late."

"Yeah, for me too," I smiled, and Diana laughed with me. She had a funny joke. "How about I pick you up at six o'clock? We can start with some burgers. I'll get you home around 11:00 p.m."

So we planned our second date, which included hamburgers and a movie. We headed to a nearby diner a few minutes out from the movie theatre, where the film began at 7:30 p.m. There is plenty of time.

When I saw Diana at school on Monday morning, she always dressed the same way she always was, in baggier jeans or slacks and loose-fitting tops that obscured her upper body. But she didn't wear her shades, and her hair was drawn back like it had been the night before. She even put on light lipstick. Her shiny, soft blue eyes sparkled like diamonds. "Do you think you like me more this way?"

"How can I like you better?" I said, picking on her, and Diana assumed I was serious, as though I hadn't noticed. Diana lit up as she saw my grin and chuckled along with me. We exchanged discreet handshakes but did not embrace them. We weren't yet able to be that available in front of the school grapevine. We were aware, and we were aware that we were growing together. It was the only thing that existed. The bell rang for the first period; I will see her in AP History and English in the fourth and fifth periods, respectively. She was enrolled in all AP courses and will most definitely receive five college credits from each one. That's 25 credits before she started college. I expected to get between 8 and 10 points. "I'll see you again in the fourth period." We exchanged smiles and clenched each other's fingers as we walked to class.

Mike, a long-time friend of mine, approached me before the second cycle began and asked, "So, Jon, what were your words to Diana the other day? Today, she seems to be a very different person."

"What makes you believe I have anything to do with her latest appearance?"

"Don't say I'm a fool when I'm not enrolled in any AP courses. You spent the whole afternoon talking to her. You didn't turn up at the student government conference, don't dispute it. And how you were always laughing at each other. Did you head out on Friday night? Man, come on. Let's speak."

I figured I wanted to inform him. I was a terrible liar. "OK, we went out for dinner and a little dance on Friday night. We had a fantastic time. We're also heading out tonight, hopefully on Saturday. She appeals to me. She's so much more than a mind. She's funny, she has a strong spirit, and she's gorgeous if you take a good look at her. She didn't have to take off her shades or adjust her hairstyle. In any case, she's beautiful."

Mike said, "Hey, if you like her and she likes you, all is well. Have a good time with her tonight." He smiled and winked at me. I understood just what he was saying.

Diana was excited when I picked her up that night so that we could get started right away. We talked about dinner as though we'd known each other for a long time. It was too easy to speak to her. I cursed myself for not noticing her sooner. She was friendly, humorous, and as sharp as a razor blade.

Before we got in the car to go to the movie, I turned and kissed her, a gentle kiss that took her off guard but was enthusiastically returned. We didn't go much farther than a few of those kisses because we needed to get to the movie. Her lips, on the other hand, were smooth and nice. She had a lot of natural ability for a person who hadn't kissed often, if at all.

Diana decided on purchasing popcorn and a soft drink to share. I attempted to compensate, but she refused. "You paid for dinner and the tickets. I'd like to do something, Jon." I didn't want to fight with her, and I enjoyed paying for a portion of the trip. I wasn't exactly flush with cash.

We were seated at the back of the theatre, where there were some vacant seats. The film had been out for only two weeks and was a big success, but it was a weeknight, and the audience was light, so there were several vacant seats around us. As the movie began, I wrapped my arm around her, and she cuddled up to me. We were quite comfortable together, including the fact that the arm of the seat was between us.

We paid careful attention to the first third of the film, which tells the tale of an Oklahoma draftee who visits New York City for a few days of fun before reporting for duty. There, he encounters a group of hippies, experiments with narcotics (including an extreme LSD trip), is imprisoned, and falls in love with a wealthy, sophisticated woman. We weren't aware of what happened after that because we were hanging out as though we had discovered kissing. It began with a few soft kisses every few minutes, but it soon escalated into a full-fledged making-out session. I even reached tentatively for her breast over her jumper, and she didn't brush my hand away this time. Diana turned back and sighed into my mouth as I softly massaged it. I kept adding gentle pressure to her breasts, alternating between them, and we lost the whole second half of the movie from then on. We didn't pause before the lights came on, and we exchanged shy but not regretful glances.

We got in my car shortly after 9:30 a.m., with more than an hour until I had to drop her off and drive home myself. "Is there something you'd want to explore or somewhere you'd like to go?" I inquired, not wanting the evening to stop.

"Do people really 'park' under the bridge?" Diana inquired, assuming she was referring to the Whitestone Bridge. There was a park by the bridge, but there wasn't much anonymity, except in the warmer season, since private houses were across the lane. It was perfect for hugging, just not for anything else. Perhaps she wished to move a bit farther..... I understood just where I wanted to go.

"People do it, but it's not intimate. I know a great location nearby. Whether that's okay with you."

"I'm not bothered, Jon. I'd like to spend more time alone with you. Only don't hold your breath waiting for me to move too fast." Her eyes sparkled, so I got the note.

I informed her as I was leaving, "Remember what I told you, Diana. I'll never ask you to do anything that you're capable of. I guarantee it." That reassured her, and we rode less than ten minutes to a location I knew of near the bridge, but it was a very secret tiny place with just three parking spaces. Fortunately, no one else was there on a chilly Monday night. We were the only ones there. '

I left the car running and opened the back window to hold the heat to ensure no gases accumulated. Diana faced me with her back to the entrance, and her smile was all the invitation I wanted. We had our lips sealed again in no time, picking up where we had left off in the theatre. My hands began a more deliberate and thorough examination of Diana's body. She also

31

made me feel underneath her jumper and under the cups of her bra. Her nipples were thick and erect, and her breasts were tiny yet tender. My left hand's fingertips played with her boobs, causing her to gasp loudly between kisses while my right hand hugged her close.

"It sounds amazing, Jon," she exclaimed in my ear. "I've never felt so amazing in my life. Please make use of your teeth. I'd like to know how it sounds. "Almost pleadingly, she said.

"Anything you want," I moaned as I kissed her cheek, eliciting yet another positive response from her. Diana raised her arms, and I yanked her sweater up and down; then, after a brief pause, she leaned up to me so I could undo her bra. Her adorable, lovely breasts were being noticed by a man (other than a doctor) for the first time, and her normal instinct was to cover them with her arms. I softly separated her arms from her body and informed her, "You have no excuse to remain hidden. Your breasts are stunning." They were as well. Pale white, softly growing mounds of light pink areolas and the same colored nipples are pleading for my mouth. I moved my face towards them, and Diana took my head in her hands and drew me to her. I kissed her softly and slowly, kissing all over and between her lovely mounds. I licked all over the areolas after kissing them, making them damp and exciting her all over. I kissed the nipples before using gentle suction on the left one first. Diana squealed with delight, drawing my face closer to her body. Her eyes were closed as she lay back, and I kissed her across to the right and repeated the process. She squirmed underneath me, the ecstasy coursing through her petite frame.

I needed to assist her in getting off, so I tightly put my hand over her vagina, over her panties, and Diana was so hot she didn't deter me. My fingertips moved up and down across her slit, and she thrust her hips up in time with my motions to accommodate my pressure. It was like fucking without the genital touch, at least for her. Our lips were pressed close as I continued to drive on her pussy as much as I could before returning to her breasts. Diana was almost there, but so many clothes were blocking her from making adequate contact. I opened the button at the top of her jeans with my thumb, and she squeezed my wrist to protect me. I gently said, "If you want, I will stay on the outside of your pants. Diana, I want to be able to touch you so you can have fun. I swear I'm not going under your pants or putting my fingers through you. So I'd like you to cum."

Her eyes were wide open, a combination of urgent need and apprehension over moving too fast on our second date. Her needs prevailed, and she nodded a couple of times. I opened her jeans, slipped her zipper down, and she let my hand inside her pants, over her cotton panties. I could sense warm Hair under the fabric and then the wet fire of Diana's underwear as she

33

screamed out of desire. As I kissed her lips and ears, I was able to make a lot of touches. "Oh my god..." she moaned repeatedly. Her hand was around the back of my neck, and she kissed me as passionately as I kissed her. She jumped all over my head and neck while my fingertips noticed how wet her underwear was becoming. The heat emanating from her was tangible. "Faster," she moaned, and my movements up and down her slit became even faster. We're almost there. Diana screamed as she visibly came, her body trembling and her right leg wrapped around my hip as I sucked her left nipple strongly, even gently biting down. I continued walking, and she came back a few minutes later. Beautiful tears streamed down her forehead into her ears, which I licked and kissed away.

We clung to each other for a few minutes, exchanging warm kisses. I yanked my hand from her panties and stood up, dragging Diana along with me. She gave me a long, lusty kiss that tingled from my head to my toes while we were back. And I was tough, tougher than an ancient Greek. I glanced at the time on my dashboard: 10:20. There wasn't much opportunity to send me off, drop Diana off at home, then get home before my curfew, which my parents strictly enforced on a school night if Diana was still willing to help me with my dilemma.


I assisted her in getting up, putting on her bra and jumper, and adjusting her trousers and Hair. Then she kissed me on the lips and said, "Jon, thank you very much. I've never felt anything like that before. It was incredible."

"It was a joy to serve you, honey. I had a lot of fun getting you happy."

"You addressed me as 'honey.'" Her eyes welled up even more, this time with joy. "Except for my parents, I've never been named that. It's good to hear from you. Jon, I know you're probably upset right now, and I'd love to help you out. So it's almost 10:30, and I've never done something like this before. I'd never really touched a man's cock, let alone anything more. I dislike leaving you like that, so I don't believe I will take control of it for you and still have us both home in time."

I could see she was upset about the case. And I did need to bring both of us home. "Diana, please make things up to me the next time. And I hope there will be more opportunities in the future. And other times in the future. So don't be concerned about my 'problem.' I'll take care of it when I get there."

"I've never seen someone speak so openly about masturbation. I appreciate your willingness to be so honest with me. I'd like to do the same thing about you. Discuss things openly for you."

I said as I backed my car out of the tiny clearing into the street, "You can do it whenever you want. And, for the record, I liked how it sounded to label you 'honey.' I very like you. I'd like to see us as a couple. I'm not interested in seeing anybody else. It's all you."

"It's not like I get several deals," she chuckled. "But even though I did, I wouldn't take them. I'd like to date you as well. Jon, you're the sweetest person I've ever met. It's still very cute." I saw a wide smile on her face as I glanced at her sideways. Then she rolled down the bench seat and grabbed my right arm as I drove with my hand. We were happily silent the remainder of the way through. When we arrived in front of her building, I could get out, unlock her car, and lead her to her door. We kissed each other goodnight with a single, lingering embrace. "See you at school tomorrow, sweetheart?" She was wondering if I liked that word.

"Dear, sweetheart. It sounds great coming from you." She grinned once more. Diana has a wonderful smile. I wish I'd seen it years before. "And I'll see you there as well. I have to get going. I just have enough time to get home." After she let herself into her home, I walked down the walk as fast as I could with swollen balls.

When I arrived home shortly before 11 p.m., my father had fallen asleep, but my mother was still alive. "Hello, Jon. So, how did your date go?" She inquired, her tone indicating that she already understood.

"It was all right. Oh, well, screw it. It was fantastic, Mum. I admire Diana better than I like anybody else I've ever met. She's special. Pretty, really clever, and a lot of fun."

"You've met her parents, so that's a plus. If you want to have her out to dinner on Saturday night? Or on Friday. I'd like to see this lovely young lady who has captured my son's attention."

"I'll ask her when I see her tomorrow. I just have one request: can we bring Camilla out of the way for the evening?" I had a huge grin on my lips.

"That's a bad thing to think, Jon!" Mom returned the smile. She thought I adored my little sister, and she adored me, even though we enjoyed making each other unhappy.

"Okay, she's welcome to visit. Isn't it Friday night?"

"That's great. And let me know by tomorrow. Jon, good night. Get some rest. Tomorrow, first thing in the morning."

I went to lay down and jack off some more. Hopefully, the next time I won't have to take control of myself.

XXXXXXXXXXXXXXXXXXXXXXXXXXXXXXXXXXXXXXXXXXX
XXXXXXXXXXXXXXXXXXXXXXXXXXXXXXXXXXXXXXXXXXX
XXXX

I saw Diana outside before school the next morning. But this time, I approached her and kissed her welcome. I took her off guard, but she eagerly returned the embrace, which alerted everyone that we saw each other. Word will spread; that's how high school works. There's a huge game of Telephone going on.

"Good morning, honey," I said softly, touching my hand to hers.

"Good morning, sweetheart," she said as she wrapped her fingertips through mine. "Did you...deal with your dilemma last night? I'm sorry about it."

"Yes, I did. Don't be concerned. Maybe you will do that for me every time?"

"That's what I'd want. If it feels even half as amazing for you as it does for me...."

She was unable to complete her task. Mike and Kevin, two of my teammates, came by. "So you're a couple?" Mike inquired. He and Kevin all had shite-eating grins on their faces.

I wrapped my arm around Diana and said, "Yes, I suppose we are. So, Diana, I'm sure you've met Kevin and Mike. It's about time you got to know them better."

Diana smiled shyly and said hi, and my friends were very respectful and welcoming to her. A few guys and girls wandered over, the normal pre-bell routine, and I introduced her to them all, not that she didn't recognize them all casually. All were kind to her, but she kept to herself until anyone asked her a direct query. To be fair, being surrounded by a half-dozen unfamiliar people may be daunting. Diana will need time to feel at ease with my peers and associates.

We all shuffled into school when the bell struck, five minutes until first class. "Oh, by the way, my mother instructed me to invite you to dinner on Friday night. She needs to see the woman who has her son so enthralled, and I quote, "enthralled."

"'Enthralled,' you say? Did she just say that?"

"She did so—a direct quotation. I said I'd inquire. She said that she had met your parents."

"For only fifteen minutes. Oh my goodness, I'm going to be too anxious to feed!"

"Does that suggest you'll be there?"

"Yes, I suppose so. I'll have to go shopping for something to wear."

"You may not. My parents are kind and easygoing people. Simply come as yourself. They're going to adore you. I'll see you in the fourth period." I kissed her on the mouth as we parted ways, me for Honors English and her for AP Math.

XXXXXXXXXXXXXXXXXXXXXXXXXXXXXXXXXXXXXXXXXXXXX
XXXXXXXXXXXXXXXXXXXXXXXXXXXXXXXXXXXXXXXXXXXXX
XXXXXXXXXXXX

Wednesday and Thursday were job days after classes, but the evenings were devoted to learning and assignments. But, on Wednesday night, I called Diana, and we spoke for about an hour. My biggest thing was that I didn't have a cell in my room and had to speak to her while sitting at the kitchen table, which meant Camilla was always popping in to crack my balls. She'd stand there with a wide grin on her lips, listening to our talk while I attempted to push her further. She felt she was funny.

40

When my father saw her teasing, he ordered her to come into the living room and leave me alone. Before she went, she put her tongue out. I adored her, but she made it complicated at times.

Our chat was pleasant, but we couldn't get too close since my family was just ten feet away. But we just learned about the basics. When I informed her that physics was giving me trouble, she promised to help me learn on Sunday. I thanked her profusely, and she laughed and said it wasn't a big deal. We said our long, drawn-out goodnights, and I went back to my studies.

We saw each other at school the next few days, which made my stomach churn. I was madly in love with her. I picked her up at 6:30 p.m. on Friday. She said she might drive to my house in her mother's vehicle, but I informed her I didn't want her going home late by herself. Diana thought that was cute, so I told her to blame my parents. I was told never to let a girl go home alone at night. If she had driven, I would have accompanied her and then walked alone. This seemed to be much simpler.

Diana seemed much stronger than she did the night of our first date when I picked her up. Her Hair was the first thing I found. She got it cut a little thinner, parted on the left side rather than down the center, and had more body, giving it a silkier appearance. Excellent. She was dressed in a burgundy cashmere jumper, black slacks that hugged her ass, and medium black

41

pumps. With just a little lipstick, I was tempted to call my parents to convince them we couldn't make it, then run off somewhere to be alone all night. You can't do it for your parents, of course. But after dinner, we'd have loads of time to ourselves.

I assisted her in putting on her hat, and before we said our goodbyes to her friends, Rose said, "Jon, you owe it to us to come here for dinner next Friday. It's only right."
Diana gave me a friendly smile and said, "You must have heard her. It's only right."
"Mrs. Glazer, I'd be delighted. Thank you so much."

"Such good etiquette. Have a good time."

Diana said when we climbed into my vehicle, "It was unavoidable. One decent turn merits another, and so on." She giggled in such a way that I wanted to nibble on her ear. I opted for a few light kisses on her mouth so as not to ruin her lipstick. Then we took the five-minute drive to my place.

"You look stunning, honey! The hairstyle is both lovely and seductive. I hope you didn't feel obligated to do it for me."

"A little something for you. Mostly, I decided it was time to do something fresh. You're making me want you. I want to dress like that, too." I caught a glimpse of her soft smile out of the corner of my eye.

"Diana, I want you because you're desirable. I told you I thought you were lovely just the way you were. Yet I'm not exactly dissatisfied with your latest style. You're very...appealing." She laughed at my use of terms, but she was flattered nevertheless. She reached across the bench seat to take my hand in hers.

To tell the evening was a success would be an underestimate. Diana and my parents, unsurprisingly, got together well. Camilla, too, was on her best behavior. I believe she had a sibling crush on Diana, attracted to her like the older sister she wished she had. (Not in place of me, nor a comparison of me.) Mom cooked a big chicken in the chicken's fat with potatoes and carrots. Diana was petite, weighing no more than 100 pounds. However, she could feed. That was everything I loved about her. Any of the girls pushed the food around in an attempt to leave a good impact. We had such a good time that we remained for another hour to chat. But we needed some time to ourselves. So, at 9 a.m., we said our goodbyes, and after helping Diana put on her hat, I went to kiss my mother goodbye.

"Jon, she's a lovely young lady. Don't screw this up! "She joked with me, in the same manner, we had with each other. Diana smiled and said maybe Sunday as Camilla questioned when she should come over again. After all, we had a research deadline. My sister squealed with delight and kissed Diana on the mouth, which I seldom received. Diana returned her kiss, and thus a friendship was established.

Diana was glistening in my seat. "Jon, your family is wonderful. Your parents, like you, are really good, and your sister is a doll! I believe she adores me! "With a chuckle, she said.

"Oh, she very definitely does. She's always wanted a big sister, and I believe she's found the right person in you. I adore her, but she can be a total pain in the arse at times."

"How could you say that regarding such a lovely person, Jon? I may only ask you to drive me home right now!" That's false. She was smiling on the inside, struggling but unable to hold it there.

"You don't want to go home right now? It's already too early."

"No, I don't think so. I'd like to return to the parking lot you brought me to the other night. I'd like to do something special for you, sweetheart."

"And I hoped you needed to go get some ice cream." I grinned as she shuffled beside me on the seat and took my arm in hers.

"That was the last thing on my mind. I owe you everything."

"Diana, you owe me absolutely nothing. I don't expect you to do something but because you feel compelled to. We can only park and kiss if you're still not able. I like kissing you. A great deal."

"Thank you so much, Jon. I thank you for not pushing or making me feel bad. It just makes me want to take better care of you. And I could use a little help with that. Sweetheart, you opened a can of worms. "With a huge, wide smile, she said.

"I bet it's a delicious can of worms," I said lecherously, and Diana chuckled nervously, but there was a lot of enthusiasm there. We were soon back at that private place, except this time we were alone.

I had filled up the car with petrol before I picked her up, so it was no issue to have the engine going for heat, but I could have turned it off after an hour to prevent too much heat from the undercarriage sparking a fire underneath the car. We were parked on the lawn. So, for the time being, I left the motor going and turned off the lamps, and we were kissing like we were starving for each other in no time.

When we were embracing, a thought occurred to me that was completely unrelated to what we were doing. "Hey, honey, instead of studying on Sunday, would you mind doing it tomorrow night? I've thought of a way for us to spend Sunday together."

She stared at me as if I were crazy. "Saturday night homework? What a thrilling prospect! On a Saturday night, this is what any girl needs to do. If you want to tell me what you're doing for Sunday?"

"Not really. I would suggest that it means spending the day in the City (New Yorkers refer to Manhattan as "the City"). I guarantee you'll have a good time."

"I don't see if I would say no to that. Why don't you move over to my house? I'll also cook you dinner if you're not too picky. I may prepare a few dishes—nothing out of the ordinary. My parents are leaving, but my brothers will be here, so there will be no misbehavior.                    Maybe                    a smidgeonononononononononononononononon"

The agreement was reached and signed with a slew of kisses. It didn't take long for all of us to be turned on, and Diana was tentatively touching my cock over my khakis. And if she was inexperienced, her contact felt divine. "Do you mind if we go in the backseat, Diana? It's a lot bigger. We won't go too fast, I swear." She paused for a second before responding positively. I turned off the engine and grabbed a blanket from the trunk before approaching her in the rear. It got cold fast, and it might get cold again in early April. In April, a freak blizzard was not unheard of. But we'd be well enough with the blanket and our body fat.

We were hugging and touching, her hand rubbing my cock and mine between her legs. I moaned from the friendly contact of her slim fingers as well as her grip on my dick as I felt her other hand go under my shirt to feel around my muscles and the hairs on my chest. As I lifted her shirt, her breasts were concealed by a stylish black bra with lace trim around the corners. I questioned as I kissed her chest between her breasts. "Is this also new? It's seductive."

"No, I've had it for quite some time. I haven't dated, but I enjoy beautiful, feminine stuff. I wished I'd be able to wear them for others. I'm happy it ended up being you, Jon. I enjoy putting it on for you. Yet I like it when you take it away from me, "as she kissed me passionately, and I yanked her bra off. Her nipples were fully erect, and she begged to be bitten. So I did, swallowing each one one by one, circling my tongue while Diana groaned and grasped my cock as tightly as she could.

"You should assist me with getting my trousers down, honey. Why don't you give it a shot? It's a big turn-on."

"Yes, I'd like to take your pants off before you take mine off."
She was excited, more than happy to begin her investigation of
me. She unbuttoned the waist with both palms, a bit clumsily,
and the zipper went down more easily. Diana pulled my jeans
down to my knees, leaving me with a pair of black boxers tented
from my throbbing dick. "Oh, wow," she remarked nervously. "I
have an urgent request to see you." Her breathing was slow and
ragged, and her hands shook slightly as she pulled my boxers
down to my pants, and there was my raging hard 7 inch,
reasonably thick dick, the head all crimson even in the dim light
of the vehicle. "Can I have a look at it?"

"You didn't have to ask, honey. I was hoping you might." Her
fingers wound around my dick, tightly gripping me with more
passion and expertise than I planned. I sunk into the car seat
while her hand went up and down a few times. As I reached for
the snap on the hip of her slacks, they loosened and fell down
her thighs, across her butt and hips. Diana lifted to assist me,
and they were wrapped around her ankles the same as my jeans
were wrapped around mine. I noticed she was dressed in a dark
red pair of satin bikini bottoms. When I had a good look at her
sweet, round bottom, the panties were tight and covered her
buttocks. My cock twitched with approval in Diana's hand
because she was so beautiful. When she saw me as a jerk, she
squealed with joy.

"Does it do it all the time, Jon?"

"Only when I'm overjoyed. For example, right now. I realize you've never had such an impact on a guy before, but you're doing wonderful stuff for me. And you look so hot in those pantyhose."

"Is that true? If you like what you've seen so far?" Diana inquired as she started to pump me softly.

"Oh, indeed. And, to be honest, I have a thing for a pair of sexy panties, but only when they're on a pretty lady. Much like you."

Diana kissed me all over my lips, her fingers tightening around my neck. Diana enjoyed it when I rubbed her breasts with my fingertips, rolled her nipples between my thumbs, and moved up and down. "Please place your hand inside my panties, Jon. You must have an impression on me. Feel free to contact me, "She exclaimed. "Put your hand on my pussy."

I had no question she knew common dirty words, but I wondered if she felt awkward using them, particularly in this case. Maybe she had to be turned on first because when I ran my hand down the front of her pantyhose, there was no denying she was hot as hell. Her lubricant had made her pussy wet, and it was getting all over my fingers. As she stroked my cock in her palm, I ran my fingertips over her slit. She was gaining faith all the time, or maybe she was simply so aroused that she did what came easily to her.

In any scenario, we were kissing all over, each other's neck and throat, shoulders and necks, and, of course, lips, lips, lips. We were masturbating each other, and both of us were crying and trembling. My hips were nearly fucking her side, and my cock was throbbing in her gentle grip. I worked her panties down to her thighs before rubbing her vagina, covered by a soft coating of dark pubic hair. Diana stretched her legs as wide as she could, her pantyhose keeping her thighs in place. She used her free hand to feel my swollen balls, all swollen with my 'gift' for her, without my asking. "Oh my goodness, Diana. That is amazing. I'm on the verge of cumming."

"Avoid shaking me, darling. Simply sit back and allow me to focus on completing this." I didn't protest because I was too engrossed in this to do so. Still, when I saw her, I saw that she was sweating on her brown and under her lip, considering the cold in the vehicle. Her hands were treating me even more deftly than I might have imagined. My cock jerked in her palm, and cumin kept dripping from the shaft, leaving her hand slick as she walked. My balls contracted slightly, and my cock swelled, which was a common feeling. "Are you planning on coming?"

Diana inquired, her accent sexy and seductive. "Do you want to cum for me? I'd like to see you!" She was engrossed in this.

"Oh, don't hesitate.... don't stop, honey.....oh god, here it cums!" I yelled as I launched dense threads of warm, viscous semen at least a foot into the air before landing on her hand and my dick. The next spurts were almost as strong before the last couple oozed out. Her hand was engulfed in my load, as was my dick, which was softening, and still more was in my pubic hair. "Keep squeezing, love. Only a bit less difficult." She didn't run away from my semen, nor did she rush to wash her hand clean. She did seem to be interested. Then she stunned me by putting her hand to her mouth and having a tiny sample of my seed, then taking a little more on her tongue when she wasn't distracted by the taste.

"It's not that horrible. It's a little salty and a little nice. Slimy, in a way. You have a nice flavor. "Diana smiled when she said this.

"True? Do you think I can give it a shot?"

"Is that true? You're not going to be grossed out by it?"

"No, you weren't. However, position it on your tongue or lips. I'd like to try things another way." I'm not sure what got into me; I'd never done anything like it before, particularly after I got a blowjob and the girl had my cum on her breath. But I wanted to

51

give it a shot with Diana. Then she licked it again, kept it on her lips, and we kissed, exchanging my sperm. It wasn't terrible, although it was a little slimy, as she had expected. However, it did not frighten me, and we embraced deeply.

"That was not at all what I anticipated, Jon. On the other hand, I didn't intend to like it at all, "She said lightly as she cuddled up next to me for both romance and body heat. She washed the remainder of my cum on the towel, and we huddled under it until we were warm enough. We embraced lightly, loving each other's proximity. As I previously said, the more time we spent together, the more I fell for Diana, and I assumed she felt the same way. Yet, no matter how intimate we were, I couldn't find the words to express my deepest feelings.

I said to her after a moment, when we were still feeling colder, "Don't you need any love, honey? You were ecstatic before. Allow me to do something special for you. I'm sure you'll like it."

Diana said shyly, "Are you talking about anything we haven't accomplished yet?" Her desire to flirt was incredible. She simply wanted someone to pay attention to her.

"Yes, I am." I shifted her until she was stretched out on the car seat, and I took off her shoes to remove her slacks. She was almost nude, with creamy skin and adorable, feminine curves. She was sexy in ways she wasn't even sure of. I kissed her several times before moving down her body and said, "I'm hoping you'll like it. Allow yourself to go with the river." I kissed her neck, collarbones, and breasts in that order. I lingered for a few moments while Diana reached out like a pet and gentle moans escaped her mouth.

Diana arched her back as I licked moist rings around her thick nipples, whispering, "Yes, please, Jon, suck on my boobs, kiss them, it feels good." I heard her usage of the term 'tits,' and I had a fleeting feeling that this lady has a lot of sexual tension. I slid off, sucking and nipping at her tummy. She screamed when I bit gently at her smooth tummy, chewing around her belly button. I could scent her when I moved near her underwear, a bit musky and salty, an enticing odor. I got to her pantyhose and kissed her mound and lips through the satin that was surrounding her. I decided to drag things out, taunt her, and even let her plead a bit.

Diana's thighs were rubbing up against the sides of my chest, transferring her perfume to my cheeks from some of her juices that had seeped down. As I looked up at her, I saw her eyes were fixed on mine. Her eyes were wide and glassy as if she was looking forward to this. I dragged her panties the rest of the way down her thighs and threw them on the car floor. I had my first glimpse of her vagina, and even in the dim light, I figured it was a lovely image. Her Hair was not too thick, and it was kept in place by an established tan line. It's really attractive. I softly pulled her legs apart and saw her lips, inner and outer, nice and even, with beaded moisture on them. Diana shuddered and moaned when I licked her tongue, and her hips spun back. I enjoyed her flavor and licked some more. As Diana continued to dig into my face, I scooped up as much of her natural lubricant as I could with my flattened tongue. Her hands went out and grasped my head and Hair, more reflexively than consciously. Her body was behaving just as I had hoped and planned.

I yanked her pussy open with my thumbs, and her clit emerged from behind its hood at the tip. I went up to her right side to the apex, where I swirled around her clit, then down her left side with the tip of my tongue. Diana's eyes were scrunched together, and her breathing was loud and shallow. "Fuck, that's so sweet," she grunted a couple of times or something in those lines. When I reached her clit, she yelled, "Shit, Jon, keep licking me there!" Her butt rose off the seat as I built fast little circles around it. As she screamed, she actively squeezed the back of my head, "There you have it! That's right! Don't give up, boy! Oh my goodness, cummingggggggggggggggggggggggggggggggggggggggggggg" Diana screamed as her legs sought to grab my ears, and she had a pulsing orgasm. She hugged me there, and I kept moving, licking her lips before sucking her clit in my lips, and she came very hard again before letting go and pulling up. Diana was shivering from the sweat on her body in the cold vehicle, so I quickly moved up to cover her to hold her safe. She turned to face me and gripped my fingertip as I circled her breast, giving her two smaller climaxes. "Please, Jon, come to a halt. No more for the time being." My fingertips tickled her up and down her back as her petite body curved against my bigger frame.

Diana sobbed and rubbed her cheek against the side of my jaw. It was thrilling to feel her warm breath on my skin. "You're such a hottie, honey."

"I've never been that way around other people. You're the first guy who has ever attempted to make me feel attractive. Jon, you're healthy for my ego. And, in all, quite beneficial to me." She kissed my chin, followed by my mouth.

We lay happily in each other's embrace for a moment. I'd held other girls in that way before, just not in that way. Keeping the others was nothing compared to Diana. It's not quite near. I experienced feelings about her that I had never felt for someone before, and it both excited and terrified me. The thrill factor is self-evident. The terrifying thing was that I couldn't accept how quickly I was falling for her. I was curious to see if she felt the same way. I wanted to find out.

"Do you mind if I ask you a question, Diana?"

"Oh no. Should I be concerned?"

"No, it's not like that. But there's something I'd like to ask you if you have time. And, if you prefer, I'll start with the same topic." We stood up a bit straighter, and she smiled at me with anticipation. "Diana, what are your thoughts on me? I'm talking from deep inside."

"Do you believe you ought to inquire, Jon? Can't you see it?"

"I'm not very successful at figuring this stuff out. I would admit that I'm attracted to you and that I like you a lot. More than I would have expected at this stage. Oh no, I sound like an immature teen."

"Thank you so much. You don't strike me as feminine. So you need me to respond to you?" I politely shook my head. "I'm shocked you don't notice. I like you as well, even more than I might have thought. This was not everything I expected a few weeks ago. This is how I'll put it to you, sweetheart." She twisted my head with her hand, so we were only centimeters apart and eye to eye. "We came because I was angry over not being chosen as valedictorian. It disappointed and sometimes enraged me." I knew this because I recalled how angry she was. "And now I couldn't care less. We wouldn't have ended up chatting that day, you wouldn't have asked me out, and we wouldn't be here now if I hadn't been selected. This is so much better; it's getting me happier than first place ever will." Diana embraced me gently and tenderly. "But I'm happy I was selected as salutatorian. The third position might have been a disaster." We both burst out laughing and embraced each other closely. "So, if you didn't already remember, I'm thrilled to be here with you. And it's not just that you're the first person ever to approach me for a date. You're a nice friend, a beautiful man, and you genuinely care for me. At least, I believe you do. You'd best hurry. "She made fun of me.

"Yes, I do, honey. Thank you so much. I'd never thought this way for someone before. It's freezing in here. "I acted as though I had just heard. "Although you are holding me wet. Before we return to the front seat, we need to get ready."

"Are you in a hurry? I, too, am freezing, but I had other plans for you. I want to do anything after how good you made me feel. Although I should do that in the front seat with the heater turned on." Her eyes twinkled with mischief.

"Is that true? Are you certain you want to?" I inquired, delighted and ecstatic.

"I'd like to give it a shot. You'll have to send me a couple of instructions. Very likely." We kissed again, soft and loving kisses, before putting our clothes back on. I still had my jeans around my knees, so all I had to do was pull them and my boxers up and put on my shirt as I assisted Diana in finding her abandoned clothing, which wasn't simple in the dark vehicle. Her pants, in particular. We just couldn't locate them. I got down on the floor and searched under the chairs, but I couldn't see anything. After a moment, Diana replied, "Screw it." "It's just too cold. Find them and return them to me tomorrow. You might even have them as a keepsake if you want. "It wasn't like her, she said with a smile. It was naughty and sarcastic.

"I'll hold them for now. I'll return them to you in a few weeks." I sent her my sly grin. "I'm thinking about cleaning them first!"

"You're a bad guy." We got out of the vehicle, and after changing our clothes, I put the blanket in the trunk. We returned to the front, switched on the car, and turned the heat up to maximum. Fortunately, my car had a strong boiler. We were soon feeling much warmer and much healthier. Diana cuddled up to me, and I wrapped my arm around her, drawing her in as tight as I could. It was 10:40 a.m., it was already early. I should have stayed with her all night.

"You don't have to do anything else tonight, honey. I'm completely content only to keep you and sometimes sneak a few kisses."

"How about right now?" she questioned, raising her head to meet my gaze. So I did the only thing I could think of and kissed her. Diana had been having a lot of practice recently, so I couldn't believe she had never kissed a guy until we started dating. She reached for my panties, and her presence made my cock harden once more. "Are you sure you don't want me to....give you a blowjob?" She said it as though the term was choking her on the way out. It was obvious that it was a word she never had, or very occasionally, used before.

"I wouldn't mind, but you're not required to. I simply do not want you to be pressed."

"Are you serious? Much of the time, I've been compelled to attack you. I'd like to, Jon. You continue to do great stuff for me. I had no idea I could feel so fine." She kissed my neck and chest while raising my top to reach me. I closed my eyes and felt her lips on my skin in a beautiful, sensual way. Her hand was caressing the crotch of my trousers, where my cock was attempting to escape. Her hands were more confident this time as she undid the button and then the zipper. Diana assisted by pulling my pants down again after I turned partially sideways to allow us both more space. Then came my shorts as she came face to face with my dick.

Diana took a shaky gulp. "It seems to be larger than I expected."

"To begin, simply kiss it. Take it slowly at first. And if you find you can't go along with it, we'll call it a day."

"You don't have to be that pleasant all of the way." Yet she grinned at me, and I reciprocated with my encouraging smile. Diana kissed the top, then the rest of the head. She became more animated as she progressed down the shaft. Then her tongue poked out, and she licked along the shaft, and I melted, my body relaxing and loving, particularly when her tongue swirled around the head. Diana realized she had reached the most vulnerable spot, the glans on the underside, when I let out a big gasp. She continued sucking and kissing me, but she hadn't yet taken me into her mouth. She stopped and asked me a question "Is this what I'm supposed to do? Is this a pleasant sensation?"

"That's fantastic, honey. As you've probably observed, this is particularly true under the chin. However, if you believe you can, take as many as you feel like taking. Slowly increase your speed before you are more secure. The only thing to watch out about is your teeth. Anything that is entirely up to you."

"All right, give it a shot." Diana pressed her lips against my head and gently, almost painfully, sucked my head into her mouth. I kept complaining, partly to inspire her and partly because what she was doing felt amazing. She sucked slowly yet gradually, then a little more. Her lips were around halfway back, and her tongue was running up and down the length of my dick. Diana was naturally upbeat, working quickly and not going too far, but what she was doing seemed fantastic. My right hand gripped her body, and my left gripped the steering wheel while my hips lifted out of the seat. "Diana, I'm almost there....oh no, I'm cumming!" I cautioned her not to put my cum in her mouth, but to her credit, she attempted. The first spurts flew into the back of her throat, but she misjudged her swallows and gagged before spitting out my cock and semen. She choked a couple of times until I took my cock and finished her off. Diana, on the other side, pulled my hand aside and jerked me when she coughed. I admired her desire to look after me amid her frustration. That alone made me realize how special she was.

"Please accept my apologies, Jon. I wasn't expecting it to be so powerful, "Diana said as she coughed a couple more times.

"It's all right, Diana. You make me feel fantastic. "As I kissed her, the flavor of my cum lingered on her mouth. "It was fantastic."

"Are you sure you're not just thinking that?"

"No, it does not. I always mean that. And I admire how you handled the situation at the end. You're both sexy and incredibly nice." I kissed her, and she also coughed now and then.

"Can you bring us anything to drink, Jon? My throat is inflamed. Water or a soft drink will suffice."

I then remembered I had little to clean up with since the blanket was in the car. I asked her to search in my glove box for napkins, but she couldn't find any. Diana noticed some tissues in her purse, and I was trying to pull up my trousers to cover the messy mess (which will be very uncomfortable). Thankfully, I used them, and she did as well, and we washed me up as best we could until I put my pants on. Then I got out for a second to make sure I was ready to go public; then I took us to an all-night grocery store where I got us two bottles of water and a couple of bags of chips to munch on. I grinned as Diana gulped down a third of her water before ever saying thank you. "You're humorous and still kind of cute."

"Just sort of cute?" she scoffed, a defiant grin on her face.

"Okay, you're so cute. And I've had more fun with you than I have with any other girl I've met. I'm not referring to intimate relations. I'm concerned about stuff like talking, dancing, eating together, and hugging. There was plenty of kissing."

Diana blushed, but I could tell she was pleased by what she saw. : "For the record, even though you're the first guy I've been with, I'm having a nice time with you as well. You're both amusing and seductive. And I enjoy conversing with you as well. You're a really wise person. It's a huge switch on; you're a wise man." I blushed slightly, and we embraced for a minute in the parking lot until we both felt exposed and excited. It was only 11:45 a.m., early, and we weren't ready to go home. So I suggested we get a drink and chat, and Diana agreed. We came to a halt outside a bar I recognized, a peaceful kind of venue, and this time she called for a malt, something I was drinking. I ordered two Becks, and we sat at a tiny table. We spent the rest of the evening laughing, holding hands, and kissing in the car. It was then time to go home. I wish I didn't have to go to work the following day...

We kissed a little longer in front of her door, though she said somebody, most likely her mother, was waiting for her by the light on in the living room. "I'd best be off. I don't want to. If you want to come over and study with me still? Arrive at 6 a.m., or is that too early for your job?"

63

"By the time I get home from college, shave, and all, 6:30 will be better for me."

"Hmmm, I bet it will be fun to shower together," Diana teased.

"There is no question in my view. Maybe maybe."

I led her to her house, where we kissed one last time before embracing and saying our goodbyes. "Tomorrow, sweetheart. 6:30 p.m. I'll have some champagne with me." She reluctantly went back, and I drove off on cloud nine. When I got home, I placed the blanket in the laundry, washed it as thoroughly as I could without falling asleep over the drain, and then went to bed, where I fell asleep dreaming about the most beautiful girl I have ever met in my life.

XXXXXXXXXXXXXXXXXXXXXXXXXXXXXXXXXXXXXXXXXXX
XXXXXXXXXXXXXXXXXXXXXXXXXXXXXXXXXXXXXXXXXXX
XXXXXXXXXXXXXXXXX

I was more distracted at work the next day than I have ever been before. I enjoy my career and the people I work with, but Diana was on my mind all day. That's how it goes when you fall in love. The number 5 couldn't arrive soon enough.

I got home about a quarter after and was about to take a shower when my mother knocked on my bed. I told her to come in because I was already dressed.

"Jon, do you have something you'd like to tell me?"

"What are you talking about, Mom?" I had no idea what she was referring to.

"About this," she added, clutching Diana's pantyhose. And though she had cleaned them, she always kept them by the elastic band with two fingers. No, no. I flushed bright red with humiliation.

"How did you get those?" As I took them from her and hid them in a cabinet on my dresser, I inquired.

"They were wrapped in the blanket from your vehicle. And has already been cleaned. Jon, I realize you're both 18, and I'm not a grandma (mom was 42 at the time). I recognize what happened to some extent, but I don't want to know the specifics. But I'm still some restraint. Your father and I are both available to chat about something. However, please be more cautious in the future. Consider what might have happened if your sister had done the washing."

That made me remember. For the most part, my 12-year-old sibling was already a kid who didn't need to hear much about my sex life. My parents, for that matter, did not. "I apologize. I should've searched more closely. We couldn't locate them last night, for God's sake. It was extremely irresponsible of me. In the future, I'll be more cautious. I guarantee it."

Mom gave me a brief scowl before shutting my door and leaving me alone to get dressed. As I prepared to enter the bathroom, I wanted to postpone it for a couple of days and tell Diana later in the week that I discovered them while doing laundry. I didn't think she'd be pleased if I informed her my mother had discovered them.

I stopped for a glass of red wine and arrived at Diana's a little late. Diana called me from the kitchen, and one of her brothers let me in (don't ask which one).

As I walked in, everything she was preparing smelled delicious. "Hello!" she exclaimed, a wide grin on her face. "How was your day at work?"

"It's a little longer than normal. I was distracted the whole day." I kissed her on the cheek and smiled.

"I can't guess what you were dreaming about," Diana joked.

"Consider this. I'm certain it would come to you. So, what are you having for dinner? It has a wonderful aroma."

"Stroganoff beef with egg noodles. I've been preparing food for over an hour. To ensure tenderness, braise the beef and cook it slowly."

"Is there anything I can do to assist?"

"You are welcome to join me at the table and hold me company. I've got it. If you like to drink something...."

"No, I'm perfectly happy. We'll drink wine with our meal. What happened to your parents?"

"They're getting up to go in....45 minutes. My brothers, on the other hand, will be joining us for dinner. I'm sorry."

"Don't be one. I'm not bothered. It will enable me to speak with them. We'll research after dinner, right?"

"For a while. My brothers would sleep at a friend's house a few houses down. We'll be on our own for a couple of hours." She had a sinister smile on her lips. "Of course, we are not needed to prepare at all. I'll get you into physics tomorrow."

"I guess I like the way that sounds." Her mother came in a minute later to say hello.

"Hello, Mrs. Glazer. How are you doing?"

"I'm running late. My husband is never able to get ready on time." "And we'll drop your brothers off at Gene's before we go, and we'll be home sometime after midnight," she said to Diana. They exchanged glances, and something passed between them before Rose returned upstairs.

"Will you mind asking me what that was all about?" I inquired of Diana.

"Later," she replied softly. "Only while we're home."

Dinner was ready a half-hour later, and Diana, her brothers, and I ate together. Based on that one meal she could prepare. I raved about it, and she told me she had been practicing Jewish holiday specialties from her mother since she was about 12 years old. Chicken broth, brisket, carrot, and prune tsimmis...all of these dishes are favorites of mine, along with as I didn't have to eat chopped liver.

Her brothers were good kids who got along well with their sisters. When dinner was over, they also cleared the table and rinsed the dishes before placing them in the dishwasher. I cleared the table, and Diana and I brought the remainder of our wine to the sofa, where we sat together but not on top of each other. No, not yet.

Her parents departed not long ago, taking the twins with them, and we were left alone. Not in my vehicle, but at her home. I'm all alone. It didn't take long for us to get together and exchange those much-desired kisses. Diana sat back in my lap, my arms beneath her and her arms across my neck as we kissed and kissed. Longer kisses that pushed on her smooth, juicy lips that were softly sweetened with her lipstick and champagne, and longer kisses full of love and lust. So I wanted to ask her a question.

"What was the look you and your mother shared?"

"That's unfortunate. My parents are also very political, with a capital 'L' and a capital 'L.' They were working together at the age of 18, well before that was a thing in the late 1950s. So she realizes we're not going to stay here all night playing cards." Her grin was both innocent and sinister at the exact moment.

"What if all I want to do is play cards all night? Perhaps that's enough for me."

"It is very definitely NOT ENOUGH FOR ME. Don't even worry about refusing to take me upstairs, Jon. This has been on my mind all day." Diana stood up and took my hand in hers as she led me upstairs to her bed.

It wasn't a very girly room. The walls were not pink but clean. The posters on the walls were of rock bands that appealed to both boys and girls, but she had a thing for Rod Stewart, represented by three of them. Her bedspread was delicate, ivory, and a little frilly. And it was a full size, so it was plenty wide for both of us. We kicked off our shoes and sat on top of her bunk, and I rolled on top of her while we kissed repeatedly. Our hands moved slowly and deliberately over each other's bodies at first, teasing each other to build up the fire. We didn't need to hurry because we had loads of time.

I unbuttoned her blouse, fluffy white cotton with blue roses, and she shook it off with her shoulders, then she assisted in pulling my cable knit sweater off, her fingertips playing with my chest hairs. It was difficult to accept she had only been with me a few times since her presence enthralled me from head to toe. Her nails scraped against my chest without harming or scraping me.

Diana drew in a deep breath as I kissed her neck and licked her ear. "That looks so sweet, Jon, so good."

"I think you'll enjoy this even better," I said before blowing into the same ear, and Diana writhed underneath me, her chest rumbling with desire. I took her bra off and teased her tight nipples with my fingertips. I ran my finger through her areola, licking it. Diana was on fire as she hurriedly unbuttoned both of the front buttons on my jeans. She reached inside my underwear and kissed the top of my dick, causing me to squirm and moan. "I can't believe how natural and secure you are when you touch me," I said as I nibbled on her earlobe.

"I love the sound of your cock," she moaned, and her language both surprised me and made my dick twitch in response. "Jon, you're too difficult. It's extremely humid."

"Let's see how wet you are for me," I said, opening her jeans and pushing my hand roughly into her panties. When my fingertips rubbed across the slit of her vagina and her pulsing clit, she screamed and arched her back. "Mmmm, you're lovely and warm. And I adore your sense of taste." To prove my case, I drew out of her pants and made a point of licking my fingers in front of her.

"Fuck, that's unbeliDianable," Diana exclaimed, panting lustfully. "You've sampled your sperm, so let me sample your vagina."

"Are you certain?"

"True. Without a doubt."

I dipped my finger back into her cunt, swirled it in her juices as she whimpered, and then took my fingertips to each of our mouths. She was hesitant at first, but after that, we all loved her musky cream together. I reminded myself that it was only the silent ones.

After that, we quickly removed all of our clothing except our socks. She had another surprise in store for me: an ecru-colored pair of see-through hipster pants that I wanted to rip off her body. Through the mesh-like stuff, I could see her sparse, dark hair. I fought the temptation and just moved them down her hips and thighs. Then she removed my underwear, and my cock nearly jumped out at Diana, making her laugh. "Everyone is happy to be with me," she said, lovingly clutching my dick.

"I do what is best for me. And I'm amazed at how sensual you are. I expected it to take a long time to help you discover this part of yourself." I was back and forth, touching her body from her waist to her breasts, running my palm gently on her tummy.

"I hoped to meet a man who could assist me in finding it before I started college. And so you showed up." She kissed me, and I gave her everything I had.

"Do you mind if I ask you a question?" I continued to stroke her, going down to her thighs.

Diana moaned and closed her eyes before responding. "How about right now?"

"If that's okay with you. Did you just glance at me and say, "I'd like to go out with her." I won't be offended if you say no. It wasn't until that afternoon that I saw it in you."

"No, I'm afraid not, Jon. I suppose I had my sights set on something else. Don't bother asking me who. I can't tell you because it could get in the way of our relationship, and I don't want it to get in the way of that. Unless it's your cum "Diana said with a sly grin.

"It's well, as I previously said. I wasn't searching for you either until we met. And I'm kicking myself for it. You're stunning, sexy, responsive, and sensual. Extremely desirable." We kissed deeper this time, our bodies grinding roughly against each other, my very hard penis between us, almost frying from our shared sweat.

"Jonas, I just like how your cock looks between us. It's pulsing beautifully and left me horny." She paused for a moment; her eyes fixed on mine as our hands touched on each other's bodies. "Can you make love to me tonight, Jon, sweetheart? I'm prepared. More than prepared. I still like you."

I stared her in the eyes. She kissed my hand as I stroked her chin. "Diana, are you sure you want to do this? Remember, there is no pressure. When you're ready, of course."

"Trust me; I'm prepared. I'm a bit obsessed with love. I need this, and I need your assistance. I have confidence in you." Diana's eyes sparkled like two light blue diamonds.

"More than anything else, I'd like to. And that I don't have a condom on me. This was not what I anticipated."

"It's all right. I've been taking the pill for over a year. It was, believe it or not, my mother's idea. And I'm happy she proposed it right now." Diana shivered when I touched her. Her skin was wet, almost hot, flawless, and spotless. I leaned down and kissed her tummy, and she groaned as her legs spread apart. I kissed lower and lower until I was between her thighs, then I got up on my knees, bent over her lower body, and while holding my eyes on her stomach, I took her panties down and threw them at her chest.

She screamed as she threw them back at me.

"You keep them as a keepsake," she said. "After you discover the other ones, you should create a scrapbook," Diana exclaimed.

I kissed her on the top of her pubic hair. "If you keep showing me your underwear like this, you'll be walking around with the breeze between your legs whenever you wear a skirt," I joked, winking.

"What if I grow to like it?" Diana inquired, perched on her elbows.

"Then you'll be a very filthy person," a kiss on her mound, "very," a kiss on her clit, "really." I licked her cunt, drenched with desire.

"Please, Jon, don't tease me. "I'm hurting for you." Her eyes begged me to listen to them.

I was on my knees, my cock nearly straight out with a slight upward bend, all 7 inches long. I kept it in my palm and stroked it a few times, causing a bead of almost translucent fluid to emerge. I bent forward, one arm next to her face, the other fist against the entrance to her vagina. "This is your last opportunity, honey. "Are you prepared?"

Her palms were on my shoulders, and her thighs were spread and bent at the knees. "I'm all set. Please handle things slowly."

I kissed her, felt her lips tremble, and grinned reassuringly at her. "I would do so." Tell me if you need me to quit, love." I pushed forward a bit with my hips, holding my weight on my forearm. "It's definitely going to sting a bit," he hymen, a little deeper until I sensed any resistance in front of my dick. I've never seen something like this before, believe me."

Diana stared at me with skepticism. "You said that you are not a virgin!"

"No, I'm not. Yet I've never before taken a girl's virginity. So it's something different for me as well. Okay, sugar." I kissed her, kept it, our tongues moving together while I pressed through Diana's muffled cries. I pressed a bit further, and her perfect lubrication, coupled with how horny she was, made burying my cock inside her a breeze. We kissed, and Diana dug her short nails into my ass, holding on tight. I didn't care if she drew blood at the time. Her pussy was so snug and moist, and her thighs instinctively drew back for me. "Are you all right?" I questioned, catching my breath while wonderful feelings flooded my body.

"Sweetheart, indeed. I'm a little tired, but it feels fine. Could you please work on my clitoris? "It's tingling like nuts," she exclaimed, panting.

I rotated my body so that the base of my cock pressed up against her throbbing little pearl, and then I shifted my hips all around so that it was scraping on her pubic bone.

"OH MY GOSH, LIKE THAT!" Diana yelled, wrapping her knees around my thighs and digging her fingertips deeper into my cheeks. Her tongue was quivering, and she was panting heavily.

"Can you please relax your hold on my buttocks?" You're going to bleed me."

"I'm so sorry, darling. That looked fantastic!" She was swaying under me, urging me to step in the opposite direction. Diana came twice without slipping in and out, and I felt like a bug trapped in a spider's web. But a whole lot stronger. And I should have cummed at that point as well. I was fully powered up. Yet I needed to have more, for the time being, passionate sex with Diana for both of our fun.

"That's all right, honey. And you're incredible as well. I enjoy spending time with you." As my hairy chest rolled over her breasts, I kissed her delicious lips. "Are you up for anything else?"

"Is there more?" she teased, her grin broad. "You're such a hottie!"

"You're a brilliant person in your own right. Simply relax and allow me to lead you, while I believe most of this comes naturally." Diana raised her hands to touch my chest and sides, and my cock twitched inside her as she kissed her lips and then her face and throat.

"Oh my goodness, Jon! "Wonderful," she moaned, biting her lower lip. Her lower body rose from the bed to meet my gentle thrusts, fast and brief at first as I drew back only a little. I walked quietly and purposefully. I didn't think I could have gone much quicker, even with her normal wetness at that time. Unsurprisingly, she was close, and her pussy wound around my shaft like a tight glove. Diana was moaning quietly, and tears were dripping down her face as I twitched in her cunt.

"Are you well, honey?" "Does this make you feel good?"

"Do you have to ask, baby?" And when you were consuming my cunt the other night, I've never felt stronger! "Well, maybe not better....different," she mused. She was floating in her head, caressing my cheek and throat. Diana was a natural lover, deeply loving our sexual connection and expressing her excitement and satisfaction right away. I guess I suspected I was in love with her at the time. "Are you having fun fucking me?"

"It                        isn't                        fucking fuckingfuckingfuckingfuckingfuckingfuckingThis is affection. We should fuck together again another day. But this is something much more unique, and you're incredible." Diana had a smaller orgasm that she nevertheless considered extremely rewarding as I stopped to kiss her shoulder and the side of her body. "I'm going to start moving forward, and I'm not sure how much longer I can keep out." "You've had me all tingly about you."

"Please go ahead. "I'm prepared to follow you." Her voice had an ethereal sound about it, as though she were on a cloud with me. I drew back and thrust back forward, becoming quicker as I went. As I struggled to maintain a smooth pace, her body trembled, and her legs shook slightly. Her back arched a few times, we were both sweating profusely, and her space smelled deliciously of erotic pheromones and our body heat. I was soon sliding freely in her juicy cunt, and she was matching me thrust

79

for thrust. Her thighs wrapped around me, and our limbs slapped into each other.

We were grunting loudly every time I buried my dick in her, her bed creaked, and her pussy squeezed me closely as if she was attempting to suck me in and hold me there. I'd slept with more seasoned people before, but Diana was by far the strongest. It was my turn to burst into tears. "Jon," she said raggedly, "I'm almost there." Oh, god, Jon, I'M CUMMINGGGGGGGGGGGGGGGGGGGGGGGGGGGGGGGGGGGGGGGG GGGGGGGGGGGGGGGGGGGGGGGGGGGGGGGGGGGGGGGGGGGG GGGGGGGGGGGGGGGGGGGGGGGGGGGGGGGGGGGGGGGGGGGG GGGGGGGGGGGGGGGGGGGGGGGGGGGGGGGGGG That sent me over the edge, and I lunged straight into her cunt, tensing my body while gobs of my cum were churned with her juices. It was sweaty and sticky and amazing, by far the best sex I've ever had. I'm sure our feelings for each other played a big part in it. Regardless, my heart was racing, and it belonged to Diana.

She clutched me as though she couldn't let go, and I didn't want her to. I shifted my weight on top of her and kissed her repeatedly before turning onto my back and pulling her with me to keep us attached. My penis was not shriveling but rather remained hard, which had never occurred to me before.

Diana shifted her hips, a surprised expression on her lips. "Jon, that was so beautiful," she said hoarsely. "Much like you." As her tiny breasts caressed my chest, she kissed my lip, smelling my salty tears. "I appreciate you making something so perfect for me. You're fantastic in every way."

"You don't know anything about me," I joked. "Honestly, this was the greatest thing I've ever shared, the best. I haven't had many others, so you were by far the happiest I'd ever felt. I'm not sure whether I'm saying this correctly. I feel like it's coming out as if you're such a fuck, which you're not. You're so much better than that. I can't picture being with someone else more than you, and it's all because of how I feel about you. "I wish I had a great way of expressing myself." I kissed her lips and stroked her face.

"Are you really tough, Jon?" "Does it happen all the time for you?"

"It's never happened before. I promise to you. You have to be the one. You cast a curse on me." As Diana steadily pulled herself off my cock, we exchanged soft smiles, all coated with each of our creamy juices. It wasn't easy, so I didn't feel obligated to get her again. I was ecstatic and fully fulfilled. Despite the condition of my member, Diana kept my cock in her lap. She stoked me softly but tightly in her lap, her hand being sloppy. "You don't have to do it, honey. I'll be perfect just the way I am."

"So what if I want to?" I'm a little tired down there, but I don't think I'd be able to handle your cock inside me right now. And I'm not sure I'm able to suck it with this disaster all over it. But I can do a nice handjob for you. Relax and enjoy it, sweetheart. Allow me to do something for you."

Diana was so selfless and giving. Her warmth and compassion endeared her to me. "If you insist," I say. But please lie next to me so that I can lick you. "Do you believe you're too delicate for me to penetrate your pussy?"

"Maybe. Don't worry; you've made me cum more times than I can count. And I'm a natural mathematician!" I just wrapped my arm around her, and her tiny, beautiful boobs pushed into my side as she kissed me and snuggled her warm body next to mine. I sighed and relaxed, allowing Diana to have her way with me.

I was expecting a cool, slow handjob from my lovely girlfriend. Yet she shocked me once more. Diana was vigorously jerking my throbbing penis, satisfying her every time my cock jerked. She was also a bit sloppy, and the sticky cream all over my cock and her hand didn't help. Then she began talking to me in a derogatory manner. "You know how to make a girl orgasm, boy.

My cunt was soaked, wetter than it had ever been. I enjoyed the way you made love to me, so I can't wait to see how you can fuck me. A nice, hard fuck. I've fantasized about what it's like to be hammered hard. Perhaps from behind. You're welcome to snatch my hips and pump your strong cock into my sloppy pussy. Oh my goodness, you're throbbing like hell! That's just how it looks! Would you want to eat my tits? Do you want to suck them deep for me? I'm already so hot from your lips that I will cum just from your lips on my nipples!"

Diana bent over me, her hand shifting swiftly and steadily on my cock while I curled my lips around her right nipple and sucked greedily. "That's all there is to it, boy. Yes, my love, sucking softly.

MMMMMMMMMMMMMMMMMMMMMMMMMMMMMMMM MMMMMM Wow, I hope you're going to cum once more!"

She was correct; I was almost there. She got me so worked up for her that my balls were ready easily again, and I churned out another load, not quite as many as the first, but enough to render my groin a disaster region. Our secretions were heavy on my dick, balls, and pubic hair. Despite this, I caught her and kissed her all over. Diana exclaimed in delight when I kissed her all over. She smiled, and I appreciated her closeness, comfort, and everything about her. Her pussy was already a mess, and the mixture from my groin had gotten all over her. We used to tidy up. Neither of us will bring our clothing back on the way we were.

She said, "Remember what I said about showering together last night? I believe we can. This is just too much money for a towel. We have plenty of time. Have you ever had a shower with a partner? I won't be envious... maybe a little bit. "Diana smiled when she said this.

"No, this would still be a different opportunity for me. We need to get going before this starts leaking all over the place." We dashed to her toilet, jumped in her tub/shower, and took turns rinsing off as soon as the water temperature was just perfect.

This was thrilling, particularly when we began soaping each other all over. She wore a shower cap to prevent having to do her hair, and I was tall enough to avoid making my hair wet. We were hugging before washing, and Diana was switched back on. I lathered some soap on my two fingers and gently rubbed her clit with gentle pressure while supporting her with my other hand. She was rubbing her pussy against my fingertips, and it didn't take long for her to enjoy yet another orgasm that would leave her exhausted for the evening. I might have been harder and cumbersome a third time, but I was good, more than happy. For the remainder of the night, what I needed was love.

We dressed after we had washed and dried off. Diana put on new pants and gave me her old pair, saying, "You can have these, but if you locate the other pair, please return them to me.

They're very pricey. These, on the other hand, are yours to hold. Consider me the next time you're lying in bed, all hard and needy. These may be used to masturbate and cum in. You can even only scent me and cum anywhere you want." She smirked, a sly grin on her face.

"What is your name? I assumed...no, everybody assumed...that you were a humble, reserved guy with a small personality. And I'm discovering that underneath your surface is this extremely passionate, almost wild woman with incredible sexuality. You physically and metaphorically blast me completely. Guys will be vying for a chance to take you out if I was the braggart kind. It's good for you and me that I don't brag. I hope you understand that our secrets are just that. Our best kept secrets. But any moment we've been together, you've surprised me."

"I would never have gone out with you if I felt you were the one to brag. I've been thinking about sex since I can recall, maybe since I was 12 or 13. When the majority of people begin. And I've only had feelings that I would never have discussed with others, not even my decent camp buddies. I couldn't do it. I'm relieved you don't believe I'm some kind of freak."

Diana stared up at me, a little embarrassed at having given herself up in such an intimate manner, even to me, when I stood in front of her and placed my hands on her shoulders. "Diana, darling, I don't believe you're a freak. I think you're beautiful, tender, and sensual, not to mention brilliant and amusing. And she's a bit vulnerable, which makes her really attractive. And the attractiveness is undeniably unbeliDianable. I'm going to have to learn to catch up with your dirty talk. Any of this is something I might never have guessed for you, and it was a really good surprise. But that's not the reason I'm falling for you."

Diana's eyes welled up with laughter. "You're madly in love with me? Is that what I believe it means?" I agreed with a nod of my head. "So, what's the deal between you and me? Could you please answer me?"

I was unsure. Is it possible that I went a little too far? I was on the verge of asking her I loved her, which I was sensing but unsure whether I was telling her too much. Fuck it; I've always been too far. I couldn't let her hang. "I've never met anyone like you. Diana and I are on the same wavelength. I like how you're not scared to be clever or to be yourself. And I sense you're doing what I'm doing, which is something you can't really describe. Am I correct?"

Diana paused as well. Then she said, "Yes, I am. I can't deny feeling anything really unique about you, even though it scares me. I've never been in a friendship. And now...I'm scared to say it. I would guarantee that you inspire a lot of faith in me. I've always been confident in myself. I had no option because I had too few mates. So you're going to change it for me. And I know it's not that you're trying to use or use me. You seem to appreciate me. Or, Jon, do you adore me? You've been avoiding the term."

It's time to put up or shut up. "True. I adore you. I can't argue that what I'm feeling is so powerful that it has to be passion. When we're not together, I worry about you. In my mind and, most importantly, in my heart." I placed my hand on my stomach, directly over my beating core.

Diana sobbed against my chest. "Jon, where have you been all these years? I adore you as well when I think about you, my heartaches. And my body...I get so hot thinking about you at times." My arms were wrapped tightly around her back, and I was weeping as well. "And you let me into your core. I realize it's more difficult for men to do. And certain girls, such as myself."

We squeezed hands and cried quietly to each other. There was a lot of emotion here, but it was still good to get it all out. I raised her chin, and we kissed in short, comforting, and passionate kisses. And we held each other tightly, as though we were attempting to protect the other from falling between our fingers.

We went downstairs, got something to drink with a couple of treats, and switched on the TV, with the news going on in a few minutes, then Saturday Night Live, with Richard Benjamin hosting and Rikki Lee Jones singing. We cuddled and kept hands during the broadcast, exchanged a few kisses, and just relaxed after the excitement of earlier. Diana's parents arrived home around 12:30, and unlike certain other girls' parents, Diana hugged me and assured me we didn't have to be separated. They said a quick hi, goodnight, and went up to their bedroom after telling me that I was going to dinner the next Friday. We remained together until the end of the show when I got up to go home. We would spend the whole next day together, and we both wanted a decent night's sleep. Kissing her goodnight was neither simple nor fast, particularly after the events of the evening. We took our time, hugging and showing each other how much we cherished each other, so eventually, we let each other go. I informed her I'd pick her up at 11:30 a.m. and that she should be prepared. She said she would, and I left floating in the breeze. We made love most romantically, and then, even more importantly, we confessed our feelings for each other. Overall, it was a fantastic night.

We were doomed to have even more amazing nights as well as days.

The Saturday night, I slept well. My body was exhausted, but my heart was content. Diana and I shared had an incredibly sexual and emotional experience, with each of us admitting we were in love with each other. And I discovered she was a fairly decent chef. I couldn't wait to surprise her one night by demonstrating my culinary abilities.

I awoke at 9 a.m. to shave and wash. We had planned to visit Manhattan that day. Diana had no idea what I was up to, which piqued her interest but made her happy. She enjoyed it when I surprised her, even if she was a powerful woman. She was very feminine in that way, as though she were playing a specific part. But, in all, she was a staunch feminist. Nobody was ever going to handle her like a second-class person, which pleased me. Powerful women did not intimidate me in any way.

I was downstairs before ten o'clock, giving me plenty of time to speak to my family and eat something. And I was starving that morning. When I sat down on a huge plate of eggs and bacon with a toasted bagel with my dad, I got a small third degree, mainly from my mom and Camilla.

"So, what are you and Diana up to today?" mom questioned, sipping her coffee.

"K I S S I N G I S S I N G I S S I N G I S S I N G I S S I N Camila said it in her brattiest voice. I reached out and ruffled her fur, and she burst out laughing.

"That is something I can not doubt. She's a fantastic kisser. One day you'll realize it's enjoyable. Just not too soon, please. I'm bringing her into town and giving her a pick. We can go to the philharmonic's Sunday matinée show at Lincoln Center or go to the Metropolitan Museum of Art, The Jewish Museum, or the Guggenheim. Since the museums are all similar to each other, each of them would suffice."

"I thought that bringing you there while you were younger would pay off someday. If you know if she's interested in all of those things?" Mom inquired.

"No, I'm guessing. That's risky, I realize. Yet I have a hunch."

"I get how you do," my sister said obnoxiously. "You're madly in love!"

My father intervened, "Camilla, behave yourself. Your brothers aren't in a relationship. It's just too soon."

I was as still as a tomb and didn't even feed. As previously said, I am a terrible liar.

Everyone heard my quiet. Dad said to his mother, "Carol, could you please carry Camilla into the family room for me? I want to speak with Jon before he leaves."

Camilla, like my friends, was taken aback, and she and my mother exited the bed, glaring at me.

"Do you already adore her, Jon? Is that reciprocal?"

"Yes, dad, I do, and so does she. We discussed it last night. We're all aware of it."

"It's very fast. She's a lovely young lady, and your mother and sister all raved about her when she arrived for dinner. I don't want you to get hurt or get your feelings misunderstood. If you're certain, I'm delighted for you. I recall how I felt for my first love. It's a powerful sensation." He spoke more softly. "I'm not going to ask any particular questions. Only inform me whether you're wearing some kind of defense."

"Yes, I promise, Dad. You're not going to be a grandfather at the age of 45. There is everything none of us desires. But we both know how we do. She's incredible. I'm at a loss for words to describe her."

Dad tapped me on the back of the shoulder. "Well, I'm glad for you. Your sister is delighted with you. You should remember why she looks up to you."

"I understand. I owe her a rough time, and she tears my chops, but I adore the little brat." I grinned when I said it; dad understood how similar we were about our age gap.

"You should probably finish your meal. And what about Jon? Tonight is 11 p.m. Tomorrow is the first day of school."

"I understand, Dad. And what about your father? Thank you." He grinned and informed Mom and Camilla they were welcome to return. I finished my meal, washed my bowl, and went to finish getting dressed. I was dressed in brown slacks, a red pullover jumper over a white button-down shirt with the collar unbuttoned, and black sneakers. I had advised Diana to dress up a little, and she had done the same.

Camilla came by and said, "Jon?" as I was putting on some cologne.

"Are you sure, sis?"

"I'm delighted for you. Diana appeals to me. I adore you."

That moved me. She was a true sweetheart. My sister embraced me as I kissed the top of her head with my arms outstretched. "I adore you as well, sis. Hey, you remember you should still come to me if you need a big brother, don't you?"

"Then you should come to me whenever you need your little sister," she added, nodding her head. We all laughed.

"Okay, I need to get moving. Maybe you will join us for a movie next weekend. How does it feel to you?"

"Are you sure?"

"Honestly. Whether we can figure that out."

She kissed my face and hugged me again before leaving. I knew Diana wouldn't mind if we brought my sister along once in a while. Maybe also her children, but I doubted 15-year-old boys might want to join us.

I arrived at Diana's just before 11 a.m., and she was waiting for me outside. I couldn't tell what she was wearing under her scarf, but it was a dress or shirt. Her legs were in black hose, and she was wearing a small, chunky heel that she could stroll around the city in. Her thighs looked fantastic in black nylon. I began to get out of my car to come around and unlock the lock, but she motioned for me to remain inside. She came in, and we kissed a good yet short embrace. "Hello, honey. I was missing you."

"What has happened after last night? That's wonderful. I missed you as well. I had a variety of thoughts concerning you."

"I was thinking of you as well when I fall asleep. You did a good job of draining me. "As I drove towards Manhattan, I said with a smile.

"You still take really good care of me. So I'm no longer achy. Thank you once again for having such a memorable moment. I was a little worried about how my first time would go. But it turns out that with the right guy, it can be lovely."

"And you think I'm adorable. You're delectable. I just wish I could have stayed up all night with you."

"I hope so. The ideal way to finish a night together. Jon, I adore you." Diana said it as though she was afraid I wouldn't react. There's no way.

"I adore you as well, honey. My family is well aware of this." She raised an eyebrow, so I told her what happened before and during breakfast that morning, including how my sister behaved while I was getting dressed. "She's completely smitten with you.

I think it's okay with you if we take her to the cinema next weekend."

"There is no issue at all. I've never got a younger sibling to spoil. I'm not bothered in the least as long as it's only once and a while. I still have my requirements." She shuffled closer to me (this was before seatbelts were required), and I wrapped my right arm around her. "So, where are we headed?"

"I was going to send you a selection. We might go to the Lincoln Center Philharmonic, the Guggenheim, the Metropolitan Museum of Art, or the Jewish Museum. Choose the poison. Or do you have a preference, or is there another option?"

"Do you like classics like art museums and symphonies? I never believed something. I adore them all. What about music or sculpture... how about the Guggenheim? I've never been there before." It has been determined.

We listened to a Simon and Garfunkle tape on my 8-track (!) and sang along. I have a golden, unremarkable voice, but Diana had a beautiful, gentle voice that was ideal for the mellow sounds of the two Queens legends. It was a lot of fun playing together and singing together. Almost everything we did together was enjoyable.

I stopped on the street by the museum, and since we were students in the NYC school system, we got in for free. We walked through the curved halls of one of the city's most famous landmark structures, which housed galleries of drawings and halls of statues and sculptures, discussing what we read on plaques describing the works and the artists. Diana's coat was open, and I noticed she was dressed in a plaid red and black short skirt with a black jumper that hugged her body in a way that her school clothes never did. As we walked through a corridor connecting the exhibits, I said to her, "You should dress more casually. You have a wonderful sense of design. Sexy and astute. Let everyone's eyes bulge out of their sockets."

She took my arm in hers, and we turned to face each other. Diana said, "You're staring at me a little too long." "Is it for me or for you to have bragging rights? You're making out with this hot girl that no one knows about." Her pupils were piercing me.

"Do you think that about me? That I'm such a jerk? After everything we've expressed individually, not only sex but from the depths of our souls? And after I told my family about my feelings for you?" I was in a lot of pain.

"No, it does not. That does not hold water for me. I'm sure you're right, Jon." She guided me to a table, where we stood and turned to face each other. "I'm sorry for even suggesting it. I'm not used to being a part of anything with another individual. I'm also figuring out who to believe without reservation." She held my hands in hers and kissed me right in front of a crowd of people. "Please accept my apologies, Jon."

"You owe me no apologies. That's as much on me as it is on you. I didn't think about how new this is for you. It's also new to me. Until now, my relationships, if you can call them that, have all been casual. You're the first lady I've taken a genuine interest in. And I'm head over heels in love with you. Unquestionably."

"I adore you as well." My embrace, this time deeper and longer. A pair of elderly citizens passed by and cleared their throats, obviously disgusted by our public show of love. We both smiled softly and tapped each other on the back of the head. "Is there some way we can move out of here? I realize it's too early for dinner, so I'm hungry. Besides, I want to be able to kiss you whenever and wherever I want without the disapproval of an ancient fossil. "She spoke more loudly than appropriate. We both chuckled so much that our laughter could be heard in the exhibition hall.

"Sure thing, honey. Let's get these stuffed shirts out of here." We moved briskly towards the exit and out into the sunny, colder lane, holding hands. We dashed through Fifth Avenue to Central Park, where stalls were selling hot dogs and pretzels. I got us

97

some hot pretzels and some sodas, and we sat on a park bench on a beautiful early spring day, eating and drinking and enjoying each other's company. It was a beautiful early afternoon. And I was with this incredible girl. Life was wonderful.

We went for a stroll around the park after we ended our snack. Back then, Central Park didn't have the highest credibility at night, but throughout the day, along 5th Avenue, there were loads of cops, and we were completely secure. Diana had my arm around her, and we spoke about everything. I asked her if we were going to our prom at one stage. We hadn't yet brought it up before then.

"I was curious if you were going to ask me, you huge dope," she said with a smile. "I'd like to go, but do you?"

"Now that I have somebody extraordinary to take, I do. I didn't want to go on a casual date. I decided to travel with somebody special to me. Preferably, somebody I care for." I kissed her soft lips, which were sweet even in the afternoon chill. "It'll be here in five weeks. I have plenty of time to get a tux, but do you have time to get a dress?"

"What about me? I order off the shelf. You hardly require modifications on a dress while you're this petite." Eve cupped my face in her palms, kissed me, and said, "Sweetheart, I adore you. Too much to tell." "I wish we could make love right now," she said, her eyes dreamy.

"I understand how you do. That's not going to happen. I can't afford a hotel room in this area."

"I believe I will. I'll take care of it."

"Come on, Diana. The rooms in this area are very pricey. As in, very costly."

"I want you, Jon, and I said I could handle it. Can you take me up on it or not?"

I had a brief idea. It was 3:30 a.m., and we had to be back by 11 a.m. There will be enough time for a light dinner afterward. Or maybe we'd miss dinner. "All right, let's go."

We dashed to my car and sped down to 59th and 5th, the Central Park South intersection. The Plaza, The Essex House, and The Pierre are only a few examples (that one was way too expensive). I parked on 58th Street, and Diana and I went to the Plaza, where Diana used a credit card to book a space on the 5th floor. I didn't intend to be here when the day began.

I asked her when we were alone inside the room after we had taken off our coats. "Not that I'm not thankful, but how can you afford this, honey? Can you fall into trouble with your parents?"

"First and foremost, we don't have to be concerned with my parents. As you know from last night, my mom realizes we've been intimate, and I'm sure my father does as well, only in a remote sense. They were still living together when they were our age, as I previously said. Second, this is my money and my bill, and I can do anything I want about it. My grandmother left my brothers and me $100,000 each, most of which was kept in confidence until we reached 21, but she gave us access to 25,000 when we turned 18. But I placed $3,000 into a savings account to cover a credit cap, and I pay that off when I use it. And I decided to put it to work right away. "I'm with you." She slipped into my embrace, seamlessly fitting in, and we exchanged a slew of passionate kisses. Short kisses, long and sensual kisses, intense and passionate kisses We exchanged a slew of kisses as our bodies brushed against each other.

I stroked my fingertips through her thick hair and said, "If I had known you were going to be rich, I might have asked you out a long time ago," before raising my brows lecherously.

"Wow, you're one of my dreams." A gypsy. So, if you're going to be my hired stud, you'll have to strip. "Please hurry!" Diana sat in a big chair by the bed, a filthy grin on her face and her legs crossed provocatively. She needed to have fun. Her sexuality was amazing.

I noticed the radio in the room and turned on a sexy R&B channel. As the music and the male singer performed, I pulled my jacket over my head and slowly unbuttoned my top, trying to project a calm, sexy grin. "Stay with me, Stud. "I'd like to see more skin!" Diana was having a great time. Who knows what dreams anyone else has in their heads?

I took off my shirt and threw it to her, and she laughed sexily and nervously. "Are you pleased with what you've seen so far, lady?" "Am I what you were expecting today?"

"Eh, you'll do," she said, somewhat busting my balls. It was amusing and flirtatious. "Let's see how you fit about the majority of it." "I want to have my money's worth!"

I unbuttoned the front of my trousers one at a time, one foot or so in front of her ears. Diana's eyes alternated between staring at my forehead and then at my groin. I pulled my jeans down over my hips and down my thighs, leaving me with only my black underwear. Diana was aroused, as shown by the expression on her forehead. I believe she licked her lips involuntarily. She then put her palms on my hips and slid them all over my lower body. She felt my cock, then my legs, taking her time. She ran her hands across my stomach and ribs until they eventually reached my throbbing hard dick, which was only barely concealed under my jeans.

"I want to see this," she said as she removed my briefs. My cock emerged, only a few inches away from her lips. I don't believe I've ever been as turned on as I was at that time in my life. I was taking deep, shallow breaths while staring at her. Diana took a long lick at the base of my cock and then blowing warm air on it. I figured I was going insane. I screamed and struggled in her grip.

"Oh, Diana! Screw you!" You've got me wanting to run out of my skin!" She glanced up at me, her lips pursed and a constant stream of air blowing from her mouth. As my cock dried, she wet it again and continued to blow on me. My hands gripped her shoulders, torn between having Diana do what she wished and shoving my dick into her throat. She might not have had any training, but she was all for fun and games.

Diana must have realized how hot she was, so she chose for me. She sucked gently at first, rolling her tongue all over the surface of my cock while her slender fingers teased my nuts. I closed my eyes and shook my head from side to side, caught in the delicious feeling of Diana's soft blowout.

When I opened my eyes after running my fingertips through her hair, I saw her eyes gazing up at me with what can only be characterized as love and adoration. I recognized the expression because it was similar to the one I was sending Diana. My enthusiasm was getting out of hand, so I softly pulled her back as a string of saliva attached her lips to my dick. It shattered and dripped down her cheek until she brushed it clean, making her appear rather unladylike and naughty. She was having a great time.

"Why did you put a halt to me, sweetheart?" "I was having fun doing that."

"Not quite as many as I was, believe me." I wouldn't have cum if I let you keep driving because I didn't want to. No, not yet. I have some stuff I want to do to you right now." I swung her out of the chair and raised her petite body into the air, catching her by the waist. She screeched a cough as though I were tickling her. I kissed her tummy and lifted the front of her jumper before throwing her on the bed and jumping after her.

"Aid! There's a wild, sexy, naked guy in my room! And he's getting me as sticky as an inferno!" Diana said this when she smothered me with kisses. I returned them all, but something wasn't quite right.

"We're not in balance, honey."

"How come?" "What's the matter?" she said, a knowing grin on her face.

"One of us is nude, and the other is fully clothed. "Doesn't seem like fair, does it?"

"I suppose not. "So, what are you going to do with it?" she teased.

"Just this," I said as I searched for her skirt's side pin. I discovered it and fumbled to unlock it, so the two smaller buttons and her skirt fell undone. Diana was dressed all in black, from her jumper to her pantyhose, with the black panties partially concealed under the opaque hosiery. I kissed her tummy as she undid her jumper and threw her bra to me with one hand. We were both steaming hot for each other, but I felt obligated to pay her special attention.

I went up to her body, kissing her tummy, then her stomach, sucking her nipples, so they sparkled in the soft light of the room. Diana was whimpering and writhing on the ground, so I rolled onto my back and drew her over to me, her boobs in my direction, and sucked and nibbled at her thick nipples. Diana moaned heavily again, this time brushing her fingertips through

104

my hair with a gentle yet sensual touch. My palms were on her bottom, massaging her butt, first through her pantyhose and then down the back, down the back of her panties as well, her warm and cute little cheeks overflowing my hands. "That's fantastic, sweetheart. I like having your hands on my body. You're fucking hot. My hottie. Jon, I adore you. "So many," she grumbled.

Before kissing her mouth, I removed my lips from her boobs and kissed her neck. "I adore you as well, my darling." I appreciate you taking me here. "I'm sorry I couldn't get you here," I said, looking up into her eyes.

"Don't worry; you don't have to feel terrible. You've done too much for me in just a brief period. I'm more alive than I've ever been. "Where were we before?"

"It's not where we were; it's where we're headed," I said as I kissed her again and moved my lips down her body. "Help me keep your hose off," I said, laying her on her back. I'm not going to rip them. Ok, I do, so you'll have to justify yourself when you get home."

She chuckled, which was already one of my favorite noises in the whole universe. "My parents are fairly understanding, but I'm not sure what they'd think about a boyfriend that ripped their daughter's clothes off." Or maybe a daughter who promoted such conduct." She assisted in softly rolling them off, and we tossed them on the chair. She was just wearing her panties, black satin with lace around the edges, and very thin. I ran my face over the shiny satin, sticking my tongue out to lick at my treasure concealed underneath. Diana's hands were on the back of my shoulders, squeezing me closer to her steaming cunt with her legs spread apart. With her slim legs apart and the thin strip of black cloth covering her vagina, she was an erotic vision. I had to have my preferences.

As Diana spasmed and moaned, I yanked her pantyhose aside and gently flicked my tongue across her delicate lips. Her flavor was rich and a little musky, a flavor I craved, and I pulled her knees apart, spreading her pussy just enough to make it seem to be laughing at me. As I sucked on her mouth, I forced my tongue deeper into her and my nose closer to her clit. "Damn you, Jon! Quit teasing me!" Eating me or fucking me! "I like, really, really, really, really, really, really, really, really, really

"Whatever you want, honey," I said before diving in and devouring her cunt. My tongue assaulted her folds and openings, then circled her clit, flicking it a few times while she screamed out. Then I shocked her by pulling back even further, exposing her pussy and rear, and licking all over her anus.

"So good, girl, so goddamn fine," she moaned repeatedly. "DON'T Hesitate, DON'T STOP DON'T STOP DON'T STOP DON'T ST "TSTOP! STOP!! STOP!! STOP!! TST Diana gasped as a tiny torrent of her cunt leaked onto my tongue. Her body shook, her legs stiffened, and her fingertips tugged at the bedspread. And before she could unwind, I jumped on top of her and slid my cock into her vagina.

She was already extremely tight, but it was a good thing she was wet. Diana was like a clamp since we'd just had intercourse once, the night before, her first time. A wet, warm, and gentle clamp, perfect for my cock. I remained still inside her, allowing Diana to adapt to being filled once more. Then she replied, "No, Jon," and I realized she didn't want this, and I had crossed a fine line.

Diana pushed me on my ass, holding my cock inside her velvety house, and I was about to pull out and apologize. I was a boxer, almost twice her size, but she took me off guard when she flipped me over. In a particular situation, I might have been humiliated. Diana stood up straight, her thighs wrapped around my waist, her knees firmly flat on the mattress. "I want to win this time," she said, smiling lovingly and lustfully. "Give me command."

"You frightened the living daylights out of me. I assumed you believed I was assaulting you."

"Oh, Jon, that's so ridiculous." She knelt and kissed me gently. "You will never do anything like that to me or some other lady. I'm sure about that."

"No, I wouldn't, but you said "no" when I approached you. At the very least, I figured you weren't prepared."

Diana hugged me with her muscles, which were strong, wet, and moist. She didn't get up; instead, she continued to rub my cock with her body. "Please accept my apologies, sweetheart. I should not have frightened you. I just wanted to see what it's like to be in control. And it sounds fantastic. I can't believe I've been losing out on so many wonderful opportunities. Still, I doubt they'd be almost as fine if I hadn't shared them with you."

We held hands, her slender, short fingers in mine slightly thicker, longer ones. Her panties were already on, and it was a sweltering sight to see us united in that way with that patch of black satin. "I enjoy being with you as well, honey. You're by far the greatest and most romantic girlfriend I've ever met. It doesn't even come near. Honey, I adore you. I believe that."

Diana grinned at me and began softly moving her hips. She understood immediately what to do; I believe everything about sex is like that. However, some people are more at ease following

108

their instincts, and Diana was one of them. Her hips swung forward and backward, then side to side, her pussy already clutching my dick. I grasped her hip with one hand while the other held her hand, allowing us three points of contact in addition to the vital mental and emotional ones. Diana began growing up on my shaft, then steadily moving back, while her lithe body rocked through several tiny orgasms. She groaned with agreement when I rolled my hips around to emphasize her different points of gratification.

I then let go of her hip and used my thumb to lightly rub on her clit, and Diana went insane. She was coughing and gasping, her eyes widening and then closing. An almost quiet howl emerged from deep inside her breasts as she reached an epic orgasm that splattered her cream all over my crotch. She was trembling, and her hips were rapidly rising and dropping. "Fuck you, Jon! Fuck me, grab me, and fuck me!" I raised her up and down on my body, sticky juices covering my penis, and without notice, I began cumming, my cock twitching frantically as I loaded her with my sticky load, my dick acting like butter churn. Diana slammed into me again, falling on top of me and licking my chin and throat. I clutched her close as though I never wanted to let her go. Her fluffy hair caressed my cheek and neck, tickling me as though it were mocking me on its own.

"Honey, you keep surprising me in the most unexpected ways. I would never have guessed you were such a passionate lover. Yet I'm glad I was so mistaken."

Diana kissed me on the face and said, "And I could never have expected such joy. May I be completely frank with you about something?" She said this as she eventually regained control of her breathing.

"Without a doubt. Concerning something. I'd never cheat you or your confidence."

"I understand. I just wanted to inquire." She paused before sitting back on her forearm and turning to face me, her lovely breasts inches from my mouth. I frowned when I looked at them. They looked great on her. "I enjoy masturbating regularly. Four to five days a week. If I have the anonymity, I will do it more than once a day. I'm aware that girls sometimes avoid doing anything at all, and I'm not sure I should say my cousin Allie or my camp friend Jen about this. Yet I'm so at one with you." She glanced at me, waiting for my approval.

"I, too, do it regularly, honey. Or at least I did before I met you. I believe my jerking off is becoming less regular." I grinned and rubbed my hand through her hair and down the side of her face. "I read a Playboy and a Hustler, all of which seem to be fairly mild these days. But when the time comes, I'll have a lot of inspiration. The most amazing lover I could ever hope to find. Diana, I'd like to share our sexual impulses and dreams with you. Just for you and me. I believe we will have a lot of fun while still being tender."

She landed on top of me again, and we embraced her softer body on my tougher chest and arms. It was incredibly caring and romantic. It was too near. I should have hugged her like that for the rest of my life. "You're so cozy. That's fantastic. "I shivered again from her warm breath when she whispered right in my ear. Diana giggled when I reached out with one hand and softly patted her behind. "Do you need my assistance in getting off of you?"

"Please accept my thanks. I desperately need to use the restroom."

She let me get up, and then, after I used the restroom, she did as well, and we cuddled under the covers in bed. Diana was teasing the hairs on my face, and I was teasing her medium-length hair. "This is very cool," I said, at peace with our vicinity. "I think I might get used to this."

"So could I, but I doubt I could stay at this hotel every week. This is such a lovely way to spend an afternoon, sweetheart. Not what any of our mates will do."

"I didn't believe WE could pull this off. I just wish we could stay the night."

"There's not a risk of that happening. And my friends will be horrified if we stayed the night together. At least for the time being. Maybe if things continue to go well..." Diana left the idea unfinished.

"Diana, I have no expectations for anything to go wrong. I'm enjoying the time of my life with the best person I might have wanted to meet. You're fantastic in every aspect. I love you and expect to continue loving you for a long time."

We lay there for a moment, our bodies caressing each other, exchanging little kisses here and there (and a couple of big ones). Anything came to mind; it just clicked there, something that worried me.

"Let me ask you a question, honey. I remember you said that your closest friends are from your summers spent working at a sleepaway camp. If you want to work there this summer? Since we'd be apart for eight weeks, and I'm not sure how I feel about that."

Diana rose to her feet, the blanket dropping from her breasts. They might be annoying, but not now. I was based on her.

"You know, I hadn't considered it. My contract hasn't even been submitted yet. It's not a long contract; it simply specifies my responsibilities, weekly vacation hours, and wages. But I had informed them before we met that I planned to return to work there. Any summer is a blast for me. It's something I've been looking forward to all year. And if we don't chat too much, I have my best friends there. And I enjoy interacting with children. It's a great pleasure. I've never got an excuse not to go." Her forehead furrowed as she pondered her concerns. "This summer, you should come work there. They are always looking for new employees, especially men."

"I enjoy working with children, but I'm still dedicated to my job at the print shop. They hire me full-time because I protect people's weekends, and I'll almost definitely earn even more money than I did at camp. More than $2,000.00 I figure half will be spent during the summer, and the other half will be the majority of my budget money for the academic year. And I can't make you off doing something you like."

We were all taken aback by the abrupt change in our mood. I completely ruined what had been a fantastic day up until that time. We sat in each other's embrace, tenderly touching each other, but where we were dreaming of moving again a few minutes before, the mood for sex had vanished. At the very least, our love remained high. It was only after 6 p.m. We changed into our clothes and signed out. Like a no-tell hotel, I don't believe the Plaza saw many visitors check out only a couple of hours after checking in.

We walked back to my car hand in hand, and when we got in, we embraced with a few tears in our eyes. "What are we going to do, Jon, sweetheart? I don't want to be apart from you for the whole season. Yet, I enjoy my work. I won't be doing it forever, but I can do it for a couple more years. Are you certain you don't want to be a summer counselor? We'd spend time together while we weren't on assignment. We should take a few days off together. And it's a fantastic place to start the season."

I pulled back sufficiently to see her face as we spoke. "Diana, I'd appreciate it, but first I need the money; I'll also have to find a work-study job to make ends meet. I don't want to rob my parents of their earnings. Not that they wouldn't offer it to me, but...my mother has multiple sclerosis. I apologize for not informing you sooner. It's early in the morning, and she has the so-called 'healthy' form. It's less extreme and moves at a much smoother pace. Still, she'll run into issues sooner or later. As a result, I would strive to be as self-sufficient as possible. I even considered not moving away to college, but my parents insisted."

Diana's beautiful eyes welled up with tears. "Why didn't you question me about your mother before?"

"Because this is all so young, my mother hasn't yet told all of her relatives, just a few good ones and my aunt, her sister. I'm sorry; I wish I could have told you. So you see that I need to work at the printers?"

"Yes, sweetheart. I'll find something else to do with my time this summer. Perhaps a day camp for the YM-YWHA (Young Men's and Women's Hebrew Association). Long Island is said to have a decent day camp program."

"No, honey. You'll stick to your schedule. I'd like you to. I can see you're having a great time. That was everything I couldn't take away from you. You'd be angry with me. But, when your contract arrives, sign it and get ready for the season. Every week on your days off, I'll pay you a call. Diana, I want you to. I believe that."

We clasped our four palms together. I took her hands in mine and kissed them both, and she did the same to me. "Please, Jon, let me make my own decision. I have time to consider it. We will see where we are in a month. If we're not having a good time together, as I believe we will be, we'll chat about it then. We'll decide as a community."

If I didn't already love her, the moment cemented it. This was what she might have made for something significant to her. The summer was when she visited her best buddies and had the opportunity to do something she enjoyed. But she insisted on it being our agreement as friends. I adored her to the core of my being. I could feel it in my bones.

I kissed her tears away, and we hugged like we'd been together for years, not weeks. We feel much healthier and even hungry at that stage. So I drove down to Chinatown, where we had a fantastic meal that was much superior to any nearby Chinese restaurant, and then we walked across Canal Street into Little Italy for dessert. New York is the best city in the country with cuisine from all over the world.

It was almost 10:30 when I arrived at Diana's house. It was a little early, but we'd had a long day and were still exhausted. We cuddled in the seat for about ten minutes before calling it a night.

"Thank you for a wonderful day, sweetheart," Diana said, her voice content yet exhausted. She seemed sleepy, but she was always lovely, in my opinion.

"Thank you as well. You made the day's highlight possible. We'll have to work out how to get together a couple of days a week. The backseat is functional, but a bed is much superior." We were both giggling quietly, and our laughter had worn us out. "Honey, good night. I'll see you first thing in the morning. I adore you."

"Jon, I adore you as well. Per day, more and more." We kissed for a long time, then I walked her to her house, kissed her briefly but sweetly, and she was inside, and I was on my way home.

Both of my parents were still sleeping as I came in. Camilla has been sleeping for at least an hour. I went into their space to say hello and goodnight. "Hello. I'm comfortable and secure at home."

"Good to see you, and right before your curfew," mom said with a grin. "Have you had a nice time?"

"We had a fantastic time. We've still done it. Diana picked the Guggenheim, and after that, we walked around the park for a while until I brought her to dinner in Chinatown, where she purchased dessert at Ferrara's. Overall, it was a fantastic day."

Of course, I left out some important details that they didn't need to hear.

"We're happy you're having so much fun with Diana. You're extremely fortunate, Jon. I assume you are aware of this."

"I assure you that I do. I'm also cursing myself for not finding her earlier. I'm so happy no one else did that, for my sake. How are you doing, by the way?"

"That's pretty sweet. I wouldn't have noticed I was ill if it wasn't for a little ache."

"Please let me know if there is something I can do for you. And, if you change your mind and allow me to remain at home for classes, I'll attend Queens College in the fall."

"We told you it wasn't going to happen, Jon," my father said from the other side of the room. "And now that you're with Diana, it's not even a query. Your mother would be fine for several years. And I'm perfectly capable of looking after her."

Along with a 5-foot tall 12-year-old girl down the hall, these were the other people I adored with all my core. I was very fortunate. I said goodnight, undressed, and collapsed into a fast and deep sleep after finishing my business in the bathroom.

XXXXXXXXXXXXXXXXXXXXXXXXXXXXXXXXXXXXXXXXXXXX
XXXXXXXXXXXXXXXXXXXXXXXXXXXXXXXXXXXXXXXXXXXX
XXXXXXXXXXXXXXXXXX

Diana and I became a public couple in the week that followed. We kissed in front of our colleagues, I began waking her up in the mornings, and we spent the afternoons I wasn't working together, often with friends and sometimes alone. On days that I had to rush to work, I would wait 10 minutes for her and always be on time. Many nights were spent on assignments, but we might get together once a week. We couldn't even make things work for Friday night that week. Diana had a tiny family gathering to attend and couldn't carry me. Since the arrangements had already been made before she knew me, I remained at home and watched the Yankees with my father and sister while my mother watched a movie in her bed. We had a real family night like we hadn't had in a long time.

Saturday night was my big night out with two lovely girls, Diana and Camilla. My sister was looking forward to going out for pizza and a movie with her big brother and his family. It was adorable to watch her get dressed as if she were off on a date. She also tried to put on lipstick, but my mother told her no way. Mom ruled, and I shrugged my shoulders as if to apologize. Camilla was too early to wear lipstick, I decided with our mother. I wanted her to be a child for as long as she could, to savor the period of her life. She was, though, on her path to being a lesbian. When she turned 13, her Bat Mitzvah was in October. My younger sibling. Weep.

We went to the best pizzeria in town, Amore, located in a run-down shopping center near a supermarket. The place seemed to be inexpensive, but everybody (almost) decided that the pizza was incredible, and it offered you the most exquisite burn on the roof of your mouth when heated from the oven. We ordered six slices (which my girls should eat!) and three cokes, and Camilla had the most fun she'd ever had at night. She decided to sit next to Diana, not her big brother, which I can't recall at the movie. At the very least, she didn't want to sit between us, though I would have allowed her to if she had wanted to. I questioned if it was my sister who was getting more attached to Diana or me.

It was 9 p.m. when the movie ended, and it was time to carry Camilla home. My parents wanted her home by ten o'clock, and her brother needed some alone time with his mother.

Camilla was in the back seat, and even though she was having a good time with us, she was unusually silent. She wasn't sleepy; she was fully awake. Before we went inside, when I drove up to our place, I turned to her in the backseat and asked, "What's the matter, Camilla? I can tell you're bothered about something."

She was still, looking down, and I saw a few moist tears in her eyes.

"Hey, Camilla, come upfront here," Diana said as she exited, making space for her to place between us. My sister then slumped into me and sobbed, which she hadn't done in a few years. Diana stroked her arm as I hugged her and allowed her to weep.

"Jon, I'm worried about your mother's health. She's in such bad health. "She wept,

"Cammy, look up at me," I said, using a nickname I hadn't called her in a long time. When she did, I told her, "You're terrified, aren't you? You're not the only person that feels this way. I'm terrified as well."

"Are you? You don't demonstrate it." Diana exchanged a concerned expression with me as she sniffed.

"I haven't yet shown it to Diana since I'm always figuring out how to cope with it. I can assure you that mom will be around for a long time. People will deal with the illness she has for a long time. She won't be as good as she once was, and she'll need our support eventually, although it won't be for a long time.

She'll be dancing at your Bat Mitzvah and driving normally for years to come. But you, me, and my father will be there for her when she needs us. We must be strong for her."

"But you're not going to be anywhere. You'll be leaving in a few months. "She said this bitterly. It was right there that was bothering her. Partly because of Mum, but also because she was concerned about me losing her. My dear sister.

"Cammy, pay attention to what I'm doing. I'll always be your brother, and even though I'm thousands of miles away, you'll always be my sister and companion. I'll be there with you if you need me, only a phone call away. I'll never leave your side. That is something I would never, ever do to you." I embraced her as though she were my best mate. She may be obnoxious at times, but she was a sweetheart on the inside. "Do you feel fine now?"

"Yes, indeed. Thank you, Jon; I adore you."

"And I adore you as well. Isn't it true that you and I work well together?"

"Correct," she said, smiling. She seemed to be in much better shape. Diana and I escorted her into the building, and after saying goodnight to her and my friends, Diana and I returned to my vehicle, where I sped towards... I had no idea where I was headed. Diana was suddenly really still.

"Are you all right now, honey?"

"Jon, I'm doing just fine. Could you pull over for a moment?"

Diana jumped into my arms when I pulled into the next vacant space on the street and placed the car in park. "You are the greatest guy I can think about. The way you talked to Camilla was incredible. You are unquestionably the greatest brother she might get." Diana kissed me all over my face, especially my lips, which were teased with the tip of her tongue. Then she murmured, "Bring me to our house. Tonight, I just want you. My wonderful boyfriend."

I kissed her again and softly said, "My wonderful girlfriend. Camilla adores you as well. She has excellent taste."

She squeezed my hand the whole time before we arrived at our version of Lovers Lane. Unfortunately, another vehicle had already stopped there. We might even park so that we wouldn't be isolated.

"I don't mind at all, sweetheart. I want to stay with you, regardless of anyone else is there. Simply park and meet me in the rear."

"Whatever you mean. We strive to satisfy. "With a laugh, I said.

"Oh, you do it all the time—my dear man. Obtain the blanket. I'd like to strip nude for you. My adoration." She finished it with a kiss.

I grabbed the scarf, and we climbed into the back of my sedan. Whoever was in the other vehicle had to be preoccupied with their own. We didn't see much except fogged-up glass. We were enthusiastically embracing each other as we struggled out of our clothing, helping each other strip. We were nude, and we didn't quit kissing for the whole period it took us to get there.

Diana took my cock in her lap, and the way she touched me sent shivers down my spine. She'd never seen a nude guy before, let alone had physical intercourse with one, and now she had such a beautiful way about her, with her love and sexual abilities. Given her brilliance, it was unsurprising. She knew nearly everything, including my preferences for being touched, kissed, and cherished.

I was on top of her, the blanket twisted around us, kissing and licking her boobs. Diana frowned, playing with my hair and running her slender fingertips down my shoulder. I shivered as I sucked enthusiastically at her hard and rubbery nipples as my hands caressed the bottom of her thighs and her smooth, peach-shaped rear. After a bit, I tried moving down her body to bring my head between her thighs, but we got wrapped in the blanket.

"We have to put this aside, honey, or we'll both be very upset. It's simply in the way. "I struggled to break loose, I explained.

"You're right; either throw it on the floor or whatever," she grumbled. "In any case, I'd like to see your body. I admire your solid chest and head, as well as your face."

I gratefully discarded the blanket and proceeded to where her soft legs met her torso, right where her pelvis and hips contained her lovely cunt. "I like staring at you as well. Your stunning features, flawless breasts, and delectable pussy. "I sent her a friendly smile.

Diana's chest burst out laughing. "Isn't it delectable? Do you believe you're set for dessert?"

"The ideal dessert. Delicious and low in calories!" As she laughed, I began kissing all over her lower tummy, licking at the small bulge that almost any woman has, a bulge that I find attractive and very womanly. Diana's guffaws changed to gasps as her tummy flexed and her rear shot up from the bench seat.

"Jon, you're such a jerk. You're kidding me. You're a scumbag."

"I hope so. It's a lot of fun to be naughty with the lady you love, "I said as I found her lower lips with my fingers and flicked her clit back and forth a couple of times, Diana gasping as her legs pulled back. She was damp before I had reached her, and she soon became soaked, running down the crack of her butt onto the seat, which was luckily vinyl. I licked up as much of her sweet cream as I could, then sucked on her clit, attacking it with my suctioning lips. I slipped my finger into her vagina, which clung to it like a silk sleeve.

Diana was whimpering and crying, her hips swaying from side to side. I was trying to remain close to her body because she was too slick. Her knees were by her boobs, and her anus was slightly open, so I placed another finger at the opening and pressed softly but tightly up to my first knuckle.

"OH FUCK, JON!" she said, her screams deafening. "The HURT, BUT IT FEELS AMAZING!" Between her screams, I pressed harder, gently, maintaining pressure on her clit. Her knees shot high into the air, nearly kicking the top of my sedan while she caught my hair and fucked my face and fingers brutally. "FUCK ME RIGHT NOW! PUT YOUR HAN IN MY COCK!"

I figured now was the time, so I jumped on my knees on the seat and plunged my dick in her cunt in a matter of seconds. She looked like warm butter and smooth silk all at once. I arched my back as I dug my cock as deeply as I could, and her pussy was spasming so badly that I could have summed right there; however, I wanted to enjoy her, and I needed her to enjoy me.

I bent down and kissed her soft, tender lips while I was snugly inside her, the hottest kiss we'd shared so far, I believe. That's how it looked at the time. I switched between rubbing against her sex and thrusting in and out, sending her a few strokes before returning to the grinding. Diana pushed back with me, and we couldn't do anything but grunt and groan. We couldn't talk, but we could communicate a lot through our eyes and touches. Our sex was lustful, wanton, and romantic all at once.

Diana's legs curled around my back, ensuring that I couldn't avoid her even though I wanted to, which I didn't, no how, no how. My cock was spasming in her soft vagina, forcing her to tighten her grip on my butt as she came again, and that unbeliDianable sensation, her cumming around my cock, made me cum with her, flooding her with burst after burst of my thick semen. It was like living in both paradise and a smoldering volcano at the same time. She was by far the greatest romantic partner I'd ever have, and I realized in my heart she was the best

I'd ever get. How will anyone be a more compassionate and caring partner?

As we exchanged tiny and tender kisses, I relaxed so that I was on top of her heaving chest and tummy. As we rotated to our sides, facing each other on the big bench, her arms wrapped around my upper back and mine around her lower body. We were still drenched with sweat and feeling a breeze, so I collected the blanket, and we snuggled under it. Diana laid her head on my chest as we cuddled together as tightly as we could.

"I love you, honey," I said, running my fingertips through her silky hair. "Every day, more and more. It was incredible. YOU ARE FANTASTIC."

"MMMMMMMM, I was just dreaming of you the other day. Incredible." She kissed my sternum. "And I adore you as well. I wish we had met each other sooner. It's not because we meet for the first time. For ten years, we became foreigners."

I kissed the top of her head before trailing kisses down her nose to her lovely lips. "We don't have to be concerned with it. We're finally together. And we'll spend a lot of time together in college. And ideally, we'll be able to get that privacy a couple of days a week. Perhaps one of our roommates will meet their own girlfriend/boyfriend and will never return to the bed."

We shared a light chuckle when teasingly touching each other. My dick was hardening up again over her thigh before I knew it. "You're a voracious eater!" Diana said this as she ran her nails over my rising cock. "I consider it a compliment."

"You always do. I crave you in the same way as a smoker craves cigarettes."

"I'm not sure if that's the best analogy, but I see what you're doing. Let me do something really sweet for you because you were very nice to me, doing such a beautiful job with your tongue and fingers before you fucked me very beautifully." She kissed my ear, then my chest, mocking me as I had done to her not long before. She kissed and sucked my nipples, and while I'm sure it wasn't just as intense for me as it was for her when I sucked hers, it felt fairly nice, bringing tingles down my thighs. As I moaned, my left leg shook involuntarily, and I moved to allow Diana some space between my thighs.

She kissed me down the hairline, down the middle of my chest and tummy, her tiny boobs gently grazing down the sides before she reached my hips. Diana licked my belly button, causing me to scream ever louder as her warm tongue set my mind on fire.

"Honey, you make me want to do the naughtiest stuff with you, all my dirtiest dreams," I murmured as her tongue trailed deeper down through my dark and heavy pubic hair. She didn't seem to worry at all, even licking my crotch. My cock was scratching her throat; right before she kissed it, she had to take a hair or two out of her lips, which made us both laugh.

"You're a wild beast, sweetheart!" Diana said, chuckling.

"I'm not going to trim it. That's what females do. Any females. I like your bush exactly as it is."

"That's well because I'm not going to trim mine either. Let's have a look at this..." Diana said in a sexy tone as she kissed the head all over, tip to the topside to the floor, expressing her affection for both my dick and me. I was squirming beneath her as my subconscious struggled to process how lovingly she used her mouth and hands on me. And she loved me in the most seductive and sensual ways possible. Her tongue licked my cock from the root to the head and backed down again, touching both sides until my cock was completely wet. Diana then did something unusual for us: she stroked my hand as her tongue licked and then pulled on my balls. That's incredible.

"Diana, that's fucking incredible!" I yelled as her thumbs jerked me too expertly, as though she'd been doing it for years.

"Is that correct, baby? And let me know how I'm going. Continue to inform me. I'd like to hear from you. "She expressed her desire for me.

"Oh, honey, you're amazing. My cock is pulsing in your side, as though it's about to blow like a cum bomb." I kept talking like that, lewd and lustful, and the more I did it, the more she seemed to want to keep walking. "I adore your lips on my balls, your hand on my dick, everything you do to me, and everything we do together. My lustful, evil lady." She was drooling on me, and it was my turn to make my vinyl seat wet. She then moved her shoulders behind my legs and lifted them slightly. I knew what she needed, but I raised my legs for her, just like she did for me. I wasn't sure what she needed to do, but I had an idea.

# Diana Love Romance (PT. 2)

## We continue to fall deeper in love.

**Tina Scott**

I kissed her, embraced her, then kissed her one more time. "Don't feel ashamed of your likes and desires, honey. We've always had dreams. When I masturbated, I fantasized about fucking people. I can only think about one girl right now. She's a blonde about five feet eight inches tall and huge boobs..." Diana slapped my chest and chuckled, then gently slapped me again.

"Oh, yes? Is she a student in our class? Whether she is, you're in big trouble!"

"Mmmmm, honey, I just have eyes for you." We kissed many times more. "All joking aside, we should discuss our interests. Try stuff that concerns you, and I'm sure you'd reciprocate."

"So long as it's just the two of us. I want to do new ideas. I have confidence in you."

"And I have faith in you as well. You want me to tell you about myself? Anything that will shame me even in front of my closest friends?"

"Sure, if that's what you want. This was not a trade, sweetheart."

I inhaled deeply. "I jerk off when necessary like I think all men, and even most ladies, including you, do. That has already been discussed. But, aside from a filthy magazine, I occasionally draw inspiration from my mother's panties. It has little to do with her. Like I've previously said, people in pantyhose pique my interest. However, the parties will do that themselves on occasion. I enjoy the texture of silky or satin fabrics or the feel of lace in my hands. So you now know my naughtiest secret." Diana was calm, her bright blue eyes locked on mine. "Do you believe I'm some freak?" I felt I had broken my romantic friendship.

"No, not at all, Jon. We all have sexually charged experiences. Things that cause our brains' switches to be flipped. You're not getting sexual relations with her. It's her underwear. I suspected you had a penchant for underwear. So it came as no disappointment to me. In either case, not really. You aren't a freak. You're a fantastic, hot dude. And tomorrow I'm going panty shopping. If you want to accompany me?" Diana was smiling broadly, and her hands were caressing my chest. She was making me giddy all over again. It's the third period in two hours.

"You can bet your pretty little butt that I do." We kissed passionately, an intense, sexy, hot-as-hell kiss that told me she was just as hot as I was. We continued kissing and rubbing until Diana was astride me, my dick just in front of her vagina. And I was tough again, maybe even tougher than before. Her triangle of small, dark hair was right there, wet from both our previous fuck and her current sun.

"You want to f*** with me, don't you? You're such a badass, boy. For my hot little pussy, your cock gets too goddamn firm." Diana had me in her grip, and the sight of her body, the expertise of her touch, and her dirty language had me ready to fuck her so hard that I could have broken my car's springs.

"You already believe I do. I wish you were wearing your underwear so I could see how they help to conceal that lovely gash of yours." Diana grunted as she rubbed her clit against the shaft of my cock before shifting up and rubbing her pussy around my cock's ass. "Oh my goodness," I moaned as she slipped down with her sloppy, slick cunt.

Diana let out a deep growl as she swallowed my whole cock. Her hips rotated in circles while one hand grabbed for her boobs, and the other gripped her butt tightly. "Yes, Jon, fuck me. We're going to look for sexy pants together. Satin and lace. Any of the shades. Because we'll introduce them all at once." I was speaking about how fortunate I was to have found her. She was beautiful, brilliant, and occasionally filthy...and she was fucking me so much. I figured she looked like a queen as she ran her fingertips through her hair.

"I can hardly wait. Whether I can muster the strength to get out of bed in the morning." We joked together despite what we were talking about, which is the strongest kind of intimacy. Diana pushed down further, raised, so just her head was inside her, and then sat down firmly. "Diana..." I moaned, my balls tightening and my cock swelling in her snug cunt.

"Just wait a moment, sweetheart." Diana moaned, her eyes closed, while I thumbed her nipples, and she came, shuddering as she clenched my dick once, twice, and three times, making me cum inside her again, her pussy a wet and creamy mess. She landed on top of me, and we all screamed with exhaustion. That was the end of the night. We were over. It was just as well since it was almost 1 a.m. We needed to go home and relax if we were going shopping together the next day.

As I awoke, the other car had left, leaving us stranded in the parking lot. Fortunately, we both wanted to pee, and doing so in front of each other was not something we were prepared for. I stood outside my side of the vehicle, she stood outside her side, and we dressed in the cool late-night breeze. It was colder than our previous visits, but it could still be chilly late at night in mid-April. Before I went to her place, we went back inside and kissed a couple of times.

"Can you tell me what time I should pick you up tomorrow?" As I rode, I inquired.

"We're still in desperate need of a good night's sleep, Jon. Take a shower, eat something...how about two?"

"That sounds fantastic. Which shopping center are we heading to? Roosevelt Field or Queens Center?"

"Neither do I. I'm aware of a tiny shop in Great Neck. Quite cool and refined. Oh, and my mom is bringing me dress shopping for prom next Saturday, so don't forget to get ready for a tux soon."

I drove up in front of her house and stopped. "Speaking of your mother, you know it'll be a long time until I can smile at your parents and maintain a straight face. More on your mother."

"That's fine. I'll slip you a pair of her pants..." We were all laughing too hard at that. It was amusing, but it also left us exhausted. Almost something would have struck us as amusing.

We kissed a few times until I went home, crawled past my parents' place, and barely had the power to get undressed for bed. I guess I fell asleep in about ten seconds.

XXXXXXXXXXXXXXXXXXXXXXXXXXXXXXXXXXXXXXXXX
XXXXXXXXXXXXXXXXXXXXXXXXXXXXXXXXXXXXXXXXX
XXXXXXXXXXXXXXXX

Since I wasn't picking Diana up before 2 p.m. the next day, I was able to sleep in until nearly 11 p.m. (I wanted it). I took a long hot shower, washed, changed, and went downstairs to visit my family and eat something light. I toasted a bagel and took it and my coffee into the family room, where they watched television together.

"Well, see who's up," mom exclaimed as she looked up from her journal. "Did you stay up late last night?"

"I wasn't too late; I got home about 1 p.m. I'll pick up Diana at 2 p.m., and we'll go shopping."

"What about shopping? Oh, can I accompany you? Pleaseeeeeeeeeeeeeeeeeeeeeeeeee" Camilla grumbled. She desired to spend time with Diana and me. But this wasn't a shopping trip for a 12-year-old or even a shopping trip for a sibling of any generation.

"I'm sorry, kiddo. This time, I'm afraid I won't be able to."

"Why am I unable to attend? It's just shopping! "she insisted. I stared at my parents, wanting to say something to one of them that I couldn't. My eyes begged, and my mother gathered up enough to save me.

"Why don't I take you to the cinema, Camilla? If you like, you can call a pal."

"I'd like to accompany Jon and Diana! Jon, may you please? We will go wherever you want."

That was not going to fit at all. "Cammy, Diana, and I had intended to buy her some personal products. I'm afraid I won't be able to get you today. Let me tell you everything. Dinner for both the two of us tomorrow night. Is Tung Fong all right? My favorite sister and I."

"Yes, your only sibling. It's a done deal. Is it just you and me? Or Diana as well?"

"If she can do it, it's your call. If you so like."

"No, I guess I want to be with you. Much as we used to."

Camilla was forcing me to make all kinds of deals as part of my current friendship. It was difficult for her. She was accustomed to seeing me a lot more than I had in the previous weeks. She wasn't old enough to go out after dinner unless she saw a neighbor over the weekend. And I wasn't available on weekends for her. Camilla wanted some one-on-one interaction with her big brother.

Back to my plans for the next Sunday. Diana was picked up promptly at 2 p.m., and we climbed into my vehicle. "Hello, lovely girl."

"Hello, there. I had such a good night's sleep the night before. "Diana said this with a warm smile. We kissed lightly as though we were a familiar and relaxed pair. The spicier things will follow later.

"I had a fairly good night's sleep myself. If you want something to eat? Do you need to pause for anything?"

"No, I'm fine, sweetheart. If you want to see what we're going to do?"

"Isn't the Middle Neck Road in Great Neck? If you know where it is?"

"Yes, I do. When we arrive, I'll realize which block it is."

"Have you been there before? You know where it is and have learned about it; I'm curious how you know. "With a huge, provocative grin, I said.

"Jon, you have a filthy mind. That's everything I like about you. "Diana said this with a sexy grin on her face. "I've been there before, just not as a client. My companion was shopping there, and it was a great eye-opener. There's a number we should do and have fun. Perhaps more than a few underwear and bras."

She said it in a cryptic tone. At the age of 18, I learned a few items about women's lingerie, such as stockings and garter belts from magazines. I was curious as to what else we could discover. Things I had no idea what they were called. Things I'd never seen before. I was sweating profusely in my pants at the prospect.

Diana was aware of this. It wasn't that my dick was protruding from my jeans, but it was a clear erection with the necessary bulge. She laughed and said, "Are you certain you want to come inside with me? You must monitor the thing, or you will be unable to exit the vehicle!"

"Maybe some music would improve," I reasoned as I inserted a Led Zeppelin cassette, and as we sang along to The Immigrant Song and Gallows Pole, etc., my "problem" vanished. At least for the time being. I was wondering whether it might come up again when we got to the supermarket. The chances didn't sit well with me.

A half-hour later, we arrived at Middle Neck Rd., a busy street with several upscale shops and nice restaurants. Since rents are so big nowadays, it's all department shops, but back then, it was mostly independent businesses catering to affluent customers. I found a parking spot, and Diana and I walked hand in hand to the shop Diana recognized.

Several subtle items in the window, such as silk or satin nightgowns, but none that would attract a crowd of onlookers. As I did anywhere we went, I opened the door for Diana, and she glided inside, leaving me with butterflies in my stomach.

It was the sexy underwear version to a chocolate lover in a candy shop on the inside. Tables of spread-out underwear and bras surrounded the front of the shop, with mannequins clad in even more enticing clothes at the rear. A lovely saleswoman approached us with a big smile. She was a beautiful redhead in her mid-30s, with a lean frame and a broad chest. Diana saw me inspecting her and offered me a gentle elbow to the ribs. She was well aware that I was doing nothing other than staring. Besides, the lady was at least 15 years my senior. But it was entertaining to look at.

"Hello, my name is Jean. Is there anything specific I can assist you with today? Or can I make a few suggestions?" Her teeth were perfectly white, and she had a big grin. She was a knockout. Still, as far as I was concerned, I was already given a knockout. I might have made her feel guilty by looking at Jean, but she needed to realize I wouldn't cheat on her. To be honest, she had to realize that any woman employed in a shop like that was bound to draw a lot of attention. She invited me, and I'm a boy.

Diana, of course, did the talking. "Yes, I'm shopping for some fresh underwear, some for daily use, and some for my boyfriend and me to play with." She was completely unafraid. In contrast, I turned ten shades of color. They all laughed at my annoyance. Diana was retaliating.

"Without a doubt. I'd be delighted to assist you. What about your boyfriend...?"

"I'm Jon. My name is Diana."

"It's a pleasure to see you both. We have a waiting area for Jon. It's referred to as the 'husband bed.' He will be at ease in there when you shop, which allows most women to shop without feeling awkward."

"Go ahead, sweetheart," Diana said as she kissed him. "I may be gone for a bit. Yet I'm not going to forget about you. "With a chuckle, she said.

"Of course, out of sight, out of mind," I joked back. I kissed her on the cheek as Jean led me to a semi-hidden space with four cozy seats, a variety of magazines, and a television fixed on the wall with the remote control on a stand. In a corner, there were even one of those 5-gallon water coolers. For a moment, I will feel at ease.

I sat down and turned on the Yankees, who were in the midst of a game against the Mariners. The Yankees led 5-3 in the center of the fifth inning. Okay.

After around 20 minutes, another man in his mid-40s entered and took a seat. We exchanged nods, and he asked what was going on in the game, to which I replied. He introduced himself as Ray, and I introduced myself as well, and we began chatting. He looked at me after a few sayings and said, "Jon, do you mind if I ask you a question?"

"I suppose it depends on the question. What are you thinking about?"

"So, you're what, 20 or 21 years old? Are you here with your partner or fiance?"

"My girlfriend is her name. We're 18 years old and will graduate from high school in a few weeks."

"You're joking! Your 18-year-old girlfriend has taken you here to shop? I'm 47 years old, and I'm with my wife because we like to change stuff up. Just tell me that's not the case for you, kid."

I laughed and said, "No, there's no need to spice stuff up. We're perfectly good. For us, this is a first. We wanted to have some fun together, so we figured this might be a good idea."

"My high school girlfriend would have killed me if I even proposed she purchased lingerie when I was your age. I always mean that. Nobody might have discovered my anatomy."

"I'm guessing your wife isn't..."

"No way in hell. Geri and I met in law school. We've been married for 22 years. And you haven't started college yet..." I couldn't help but chuckle a bit harder as he shook his head, not at Ray, but the entire thing. Jean walked in from the main section of the shop a short time later and said, "What about you, Jon? Could you please follow me?" I said my goodbyes to Ray

145

and followed Jean to the shop's back, where there was another door leading to another section of the shop. The location was designed to have anonymity.

My heart leaped into my throat as she led me down a hallway to a huge dressing room where Diana stood in front of a mirror. She was clad in smooth black stockings linked to a garter belt that hung low on her body, right on her hips. Below that was a see-through pair of black underwear with thin cords on the sides that scarcely concealed her mound. Over it was a black see-through bralette with black polka dots dotted on the opaque lining that went halfway down her tummy and covered her breasts in lace. Diana seemed anxious, as though she was worried I wouldn't like what she was wearing. As if it were an option.

"What do you think of your lovely girlfriend, Jon?" Jean inquired, a knowing smile on her lips. She anticipated my reaction. She'd seen it many times before.

"Diana, you know I find you're incredibly sexy. But this is a whole new dimension. So I supposed you just had underwear and bras?"

"I was, so when I saw this, I had to try it on. And it made me feel very sensual. If you're okay with it, I wanted to purchase it for us."

"I concur. Still, Diana, love," I said softly, "I can't afford to get this for you."

"I understand. I'm going to buy everything. We'll all love it, so I'm going to buy it. And I have another treat for you when we get back to my place."

Until I could inquire what the surprise was, Jean appeared and took Diana back to a smaller dressing space, leading me to the front of the shop. I could see Jean jotting down Diana's acquisitions, six pairs of underwear and four bras, and then the stockings set for everything else. I didn't see the count, but I thought it was more than $200 with the extra stockings. I knew Diana had them under her short sleeve shirt and jeans because she didn't come out without them. But it was a pleasant surprise for me.

After she had paid for the lingerie, Jean gave her a card and said, "My phone number is on the back of the card. I'll be starting my store in Greenwich Village in a few months. If you want to shop there, please email me or just turn up. It was a privilege to meet both of you. And if I don't see you, have a wonderful time at work." And, in true European fashion, she kissed Diana's cheeks and then mine.

It was almost 5 p.m., and we were still hungry. I asked Diana if we could get something to eat as we walked towards my vehicle. "We should stop on the way home to pick up something to carry to my flat. There is no one present. They won't get home until after 11 p.m. Remember, there's no school tomorrow?" Monday was a teacher training day, and students had a three-day break. "My family traveled to see Steven's family. I had more intentions for myself. Besides, seeing Steven right now will be awkward. He also has feelings for me. My parents could understand why I didn't want to go, even if I didn't tell my mother what we were doing today. "With a cute smile, she said. A sweet and playful grin.

"Are you certain they won't get home until after 11 p.m.?" I inquired, flinging open the door for Diana.

"In a good way. To be healthy, we'll finish by 10 a.m. Even if my parents understand, watching my brothers coming home because we're lewd will be humiliating, even if we were in my room behind a locked fence." We all chuckled as she gave a false shudder.

"Knowing what I consider about the film, I have no idea how I'm supposed to keep a straight face in front of your parents. I don't want to disgrace myself in front of your brothers. We'd have to split up."

"Not a possibility! We'll flee if we have to! "She said this when we burst out laughing. I drove back home, stopping at a deli near her house to get a rotisserie chicken, some sides, and a half-gallon of ice cream (Rocky Road!). We fed fast because we were starving and horny at the same time. Still, like we were both raised, we washed up after ourselves. It was just a matter of minutes.

I approached Diana by the sink, but after a single embrace, she pulled me back and said, "The dinner part of the evening has come to an end. Now it's time for some fun. Come lend a hand for a few minutes."

I led Diana upstairs, admiring her butt wiggle in her jeans. I stood in the upstairs corridor as she entered her parents' room, trying to find out what she was thinking. We were going to watch those nefarious movies together. Yes, really. She gave me the projector and mirror, and with a couple of movies in her bag, we went into her room and shut the door.

There was only enough room for a tiny television in front of her wardrobe and a projector on her nightstand. Until something happened, not even a few kisses, I was anxious and eager, my cock semi-erect. My engine was revved up from having her in her lingerie a few hours ago and the prospect of seeing these films together.

As we were all set up and Diana was loading the film onto the projector, she clearly said, "Remove your clothes. Down to your bra." I couldn't wait to step out of my clothes. I was down to my black briefs in less than a minute, which we're unable to accommodate my now almost completely hard cock. As Diana got out of her clothes, she was already wearing the dress, underwear, stockings, and garter belt she had purchased. She went behind the screen to her wardrobe and returned wearing her highest heeled black heels, three inches high enough to offer her legs and butt the form men crave. "So, what do you think?" she asked, her hand on her hip and that hip thrust to the left, so fucking seductive.

"I believe I have the greatest and sexiest girlfriend in the country. My darling, you are so goddamn hot." She grinned and climbed into her bunk, and I joined her. We turned off the lights in the room, and she began watching the video.

"I've never seen this one before, so it should be perfect for both of us," she said in my ear.

"Because there is no echo on these, why are you whispering?" I wondered, jokingly.

"That is an excellent point. I'm not sure, "Diana responded with a smile. "Please put up with me." We huddled tightly together and waited for the movie to begin. The first shot featured a buxom blond in a rather short dress and black stockings, with the garter belt straps visible beneath the dress.

"Hey, she's dressing just like you," I said, running my fingertips up and down the bare section of her thighs.

"Yes, it's a major trend in these films. Have you ever come across one?" Diana inquired when we saw the blond lean over and reveal her black pantyhose-covered behind.

"After a concert one night, I went to one of those peep show locations in Times Square with a pal. You put quarters into a slot, and a video, similar to this one, begins to play for about a minute. But it was infuriating. This is going to be more enjoyable." On the television, a man entered the room and patted the blond behind, causing her to turn around as though taken aback. She then let her dress fall to the floor, and they climbed into bed.

"My poor son," Diana said, feigning sympathy. "You took a hardon home with you. It will not happen tonight, I assure you." She gave my cock a firm squeeze to reinforce her argument. I sighed and reached behind her to undo her bra so I could get in on the fun.

The woman pulled down the man's trousers, and he was not wearing underwear (surprise surprise). The blond jumped on him right away, bending over his body and grabbing as much of his nine to ten-inch cock as she could. She was bobbing up and down, and he was exaggerating his ecstasy. She then licked all over his head before bringing him back into her mouth.

Diana's hand was inside my briefs, softly stroking my cock while I licked my fingers and circled her breasts, leaving moist circles around them. We were still madly in love with each other, and the movie was either exacerbating or exacerbating the situation.

"Diana, sweetheart?"

"Are you sure, baby?"

"To heck with the film. It's warm, just not as warm as you are."

"Great minds think in the same way. I like you as well."

It was the last scene we saw in the movie. We were kissing with ferocious intensity and rolling all over her room. We couldn't even bring my briefs off until I yanked her panties aside and pushed my way into her cunt with an almost angry thrust. Diana was drenched, and I was inside her in a matter of seconds. I was arching my back and pressing hard against her with my hands holding up my upper body. Her stockinged legs were bound around my a$$, and I could feel the thin boots on my cheeks and the nylon on my hips. She clenched tight, refusing to let me pump her, and I screamed as my cock twitched. Diana grunted and scraped her nails down my chest. The only noises in the room were the moist sounds of my cock in her vagina, our grunts and groans, and the clicking of the sprockets through the holes in the edge of the film, which was filling her face with flashing lights.

We continued for a few minutes, Diana had a few tiny orgasms, and she said in a raspy voice, "Fuck me from behind, Jon. I'm dying to give it a shot."

"I feel the same way, and I've never been in that situation. Turn over, love. Show me that hot a$$." As Diana turned around, I gave her a playful slap on the backside, not hard enough to hurt. She guffawed, her accent tinged with sexuality. "That's fantastic, Jon! It made my entire body tingle, particularly my clit! About that, stud." Diana was a wild child. I felt very fortunate to have met her.

She was on her knees and elbows, and her pussy, which was partially hidden by her lace pantyhose, appeared unbelievably appealing. She shook her butt for me, her come-on to me, as she glanced over her shoulder at me, the lights from the film already casting colors and shadows. "Jon, you've already fucked me. When you get inside, I think I'll cum!"

My dick was held at the root, and the head was pointed directly at her dripping slit. She groaned about as much as I did when the tip reached her mouth. We were too hot to move slowly; she was backing up to me when I pushed on. Diana's cunt was like moist silk around my cock, and we were pounding into each other right away, shaking her wood-framed bed with the springs' noisy protests. Nothing could have slowed us down, except though the bed had broken (which, luckily, it did not). Diana clamped down on my cock when her first major orgasm struck, and my hips smacked into her butt and thighs. I pushed my head back, almost cumming, but I managed to prolong it by remaining completely still for a minute. Then I fucked her again, hard and quick.

"Jon, you're a jerk. Much more difficult than ever! And keep raping my slut!" Diana screamed as though she hadn't gotten off at all. I gripped her thigh with my left hand and slapped her pale, tender butt with my right hand, hoping not to hit her too hard. A sharp crack could be heard.

"ENTIRELY! That's a fucking fuckingfucking f Once more!"

Diana was howling with delight as I spanked her on both cheeks four times each. She reached between her thighs and pushed her fingertips against her clit, and she bolted like a wild horse. I was almost there again, only this time I had to cum. The projector was already on in the background, but the video had already played.

Diana drew forward, and I drew back, ready to fuck her and cum inside her. For a brief second, I was perplexed, curious what she was up to, until she turned around, still on her hands and knees, and sucked my cock as though it were her last meal. When sucking the head, her hand flew up and down the shaft. I was fucking her mouth when I saw the telltale indications of imminent orgasm. "I'm almost there, Diana," I groaned. Diana yanked my cock out of her mouth and jerked it hard and heavy.

"Jon, cum on, cum all over me! I'd like to know how it feels to get your load on my forehead! Cucumber for me!" I screamed with delight as thick spurts of my cum jetted out from my dick, splattering her forehead. It covered her nose, right eye, jaw, and cheek. I squeezed my ass cheeks and dribbled a little more on her palm, which she licked up greedily. For the umpteenth time, I wondered, "Who is this beautiful, dirty girl?" And I figured it was the last time I'd inquire. From that night on, I was just going to be thankful.

Diana licked the remnants off my head and shaft, preventing my semen from leaking on her bedspread. Then she smiled at me, a sexy yet slightly goofy smile that was amazingly adorable. My legs ached, and my breathing was labored, but I drew her up to me and kissed her with all the love in my core, cum covered face and all. Cum was smearing on both of our lips, and none of us cared. Cum got into my mouth, and I didn't care. I was ready to hold her before the sun came up.

After a few moments, we broke our kiss and shifted onto our backs on the bed, relieving the strain on our bodies. We became sticky all over and then lay there peacefully after turning off the projector. We were tenderly embracing, sticky from the afterglow of our crazy fuck.

"Honey, you're a kinky kid. And that's a win-win situation for all of us."

"You hold up well. Don't we make a perfect couple?" Diana's statement was more of a statement than a challenge.

"We do. And we didn't need the movie to have a good time." I drew her tighter to me, and we kissed gently, romantically.

"Who is Jon?"

"Are you sure, honey?"

"Do you mind if I take this outfit off? I've been in it for hours, and it's starting to get clingy."

"Sure thing, honey. You do not need to query me. Can we take a bath? I'm breaking out in a cold sweat."

"Yes, let's get this thing washed up. I'll be there in a couple of minutes if you launch the shower."

I went to the shower, peed, and turned on the tap, making it hot but not scalding. Diana walked in a couple of minutes later, using the bathroom when I was in the tub (another boundary broken), but luckily did not flush. Then my lovely girlfriend joined me in the bathroom. "Hello, sexy one." She embraced me before entering the spray.

"Hello, lovely." We were both under the showerhead, embracing passionately while our bodies glistened in the heavy, flowing water. We soaped each other clean, loving the sensation of touching and being kissed with slick fingertips and palms, and it wasn't long until we were turned on again. Diana's nipples were erect, even in hot water, and when I reached her between her thighs, she was damp in a way that had nothing to do with water. We let the water run down our freshly washed bodies, and I rubbed my fingertips around her slit and her clit while she stroked me with her warm, soapy side. Our free hands wrapped around each other's backs while the fronts of our bodies brushed into each other. We were scorching in more ways than one.

As Diana moaned, I kissed the side of her neck and around her shoulder. She was kissing my chest and licking around my breasts with her lips. We were still on the verge of cumming again, and when it did, we felt a certain kind of warmth wrap around us. Her hips jerked hard on my toes, and I came in, weaker than before, yet with a thoroughly fulfilling orgasm that washed away.

We gripped each other tightly, her tiny breasts on my stomach, her lips on my ear, and I kissed the top of her head. Since the hot water was running low, we turned it off and dried ourselves. Much of this occurred without anyone doing something, as though we understood instinctively what to do and when. We were a natural match in every sense.

We returned to Diana's bedroom nude, and I put on my clothes, hoping I had fresh panties, while she dressed casually in shorts and a tee. She hid her lingerie in her closet, her fresh panties in a hamper, and the now-very-worn stocking package in a hamper so she could hand wash them when she had the opportunity. We put the television and projector aside, and she carefully placed the movies right where they belonged. We then went downstairs. Again, it all unfolded in the space of a few sentences. We weren't awkward; in reality, we were totally at home with each other.

"Would you like some ice cream?" Diana inquired from the kitchen. It was almost ten o'clock, so I wasn't in a hurry to go. I said I would, so we got some bowls and spoons and helped ourselves to ridiculously big servings of food as well as a couple of cups of cold water before sitting on the sofa to watch some tv. Diana laid back against me as we fed, as though we were a couple truly in love and completely at ease. When we were done, she took the bowls away, and we cuddled together, watching some unremembered film.

Her family arrived home around 11 a.m., and I thought it was my cue to get moving. Diana walked me to the house, helped me put on my hat, and joined me outside to say goodnight. She jumped into my arms before I could kiss her, shivering slightly from the cold night. "Do you ever get the impression that we're moving so quickly, Jon? Even if we were in love so quickly?"

"Maybe when we first mentioned we loved each other because I'd never thought that way for someone before. How can I realize this is what love is going to feel like? But I'm well past the stage now. There's no doubt about it: I adore you. Honey, you're everything to me."

"Sweetheart, I'm happy you feel that way. I'm afraid at times, and I'm worried you'll like your independence when we get to Binghamton."

"I've had my ostensible rights. This is much superior. Will you require your freedom? I'm the first person you've ever been with, let alone dated. Do you want to go to college with me?" I was scared at this stage.

"Certainly not! Not, Jon." I took a deep breath and exhaled heavily. "I've got just what I'm looking for right now. I just assumed that because you're a male, you'd like all of your doors open. Don't pay attention to me. I'm such a stupid little kid."

I kept her at arm's length and stared into her mind, always fearful. "Honey, please. We can't predict what will happen in the coming years. I just know I love you and don't want to let you down. You are by far the greatest thing that has ever happened to me.

Along with my family, I believe I am the best guy." Then I kissed her, a long, sweet kiss. Some of her neighbors who happened to be staring out their windows may have noticed us, so we didn't notice. Kissing Diana made me feel much too good to notice. "And you are not a silly teen.' You're an amazing lady."

Diana grinned and gripped my hand. "Will we see each other tomorrow?" she inquired, her voice trembling. If we had been isolated...

"We could hang out throughout the day, but I have a dinner plan. She's lovely, standing 5 foot 11 and 12 years old. And she's still experiencing separation anxiety."

Diana cracked a grin. "The poor lady. I wish my brothers had expressed their feelings over my departure. I believe they can't wait on the outside, but they're tense on the inside. We're not as loyal as you are to Camilla, but we get along well. Perhaps I can remove them as well. We don't speak much. Twins are complicated when they keep their emotions hidden from one another." We kissed once more. It was time to go. "Should I visit you? May we go easy on Camilla, and then I can go home?"

"Sure thing. About noon? We'll both have lunch together. Camilla would be out for the whole day. We'll be on our own."

That was resolved, and we kissed again until she saw me walk down the road to my vehicle. Leaving Diana was often the most difficult aspect of our relationship. The fact that we had such a wonderful day together made things much more difficult to say goodnight.

XXXXXXXXXXXXXXXXXXXXXXXXXXXXXXXXXXXXXXXXXXXXX
XXXXXXXXXXXXXXXXXXXXXXXXXXXXXXXXXXXXXXXXXXXXX
XXXXXXXXXXXXXXXXXXXX

Diana came over for lunch, and since Camilla was at a friend's house (due home by 6) and my parents were still at college, we had our first alone time in my room after we ate. We took our time and moved at a leisurely pace. I made her lie on her tummy and licked her from the back of her neck down along her spine, right to where her cheeks started, while we were nude save for a fresh pair of orange lace tanga panties Diana had purchased the day before. I could sense her trembling with lustful need.

"Sweetheart, that's great," she said, just audible above a whisper. I had a mellow Elton John album playing in the background, and the atmosphere was perfect for this romantic loving. I kissed each cheek several times before going down her thighs, both of them, first the left and then the right. Diana seemed to be both calm and turned on.

"I'm happy you're having fun doing it. There will be plenty to follow." I took a pillow and pushed it under her hips, lifting her ass in the air, before pushing her legs wide apart.

"I hope I know what you're going to do next," Diana said, her voice lustful and husky. She simply relaxed her body and waited for the fun to begin. I slid between her knees, my head between her thighs. I kissed the insides of her smooth, hard muscles before moving on to her vagina. It was right in front of me, and I took a sequence of long licks that made Diana groan and shake her thighs.

Diana was scaling the ladder to her climax as I flicked my tongue up and down her slit, often swift and strong, sometimes sluggish and gentle, my nose between her cheeks. I drew her lips apart with my fingertips, and there, above or below from this vantage point, her pink entry was her round little clit, requiring my focus. I lowered my position and lashed her pleasure core with thick, wet strokes. Diana was pulling back at me, and her cunt was all over my nose, spraying me with her delectable perfume. She screamed as I continued my attack, mixing short licks with sucks as my lips caught the little pebble and tugged tight. "Suck me, kid! Suck my vagina, do whatever you want as long as you don't stop!" I worked one, then two fingers into her pussy while working her clit, and Diana came, then came again, and again

163

before she begged me to quit. I enabled her to come down gently.

Diana was now lying face down and unable to breathe. My fingertips gently brushed her back, up and down her arm, up to the back of her collar, and finally along the base of her spine at the bottom. She shivered, not because she was freezing, but because of what was going on in her body. "You're the finest, sweetheart," she said solemnly.

"How do you know? I'm your only specimen. "I made a joke.

"I don't believe I want any more. If there's a better man out there, another lady should have him. I've found just what I'm looking for right now." She rolled over, and I was treated to a view of her lovely body, from the sexy curve where her legs meet her torso, up her flat tummy to her tiny, round breasts, back up to her neck and shoulders, and, of course, her lovely face. I fell madly in love with her in a really short period. We were either insane, or this was the real thing.

"I'm pretty pleased as well. All I need is right here. "I kissed her, then gently bit her shoulder. I softly squeezed her butt, feeling her smooth, light peach fuzz hairs there. She laughed and pressed my head into hers. Diana then pulled me against the wall and kissed my lips. "It's my turn to look after you."

"Only if you insist," I said as I leaned up against the headboard, and Diana sat between my thighs. She lowered her head and kissed my balls as her palm cradled my cock and her thumb rubbed my glans lazily. Diana grinned widely as my body spasmed as a result of her behavior.

"I hope I found something you'll want!" Diana said, chuckling. She placed her thumb in her cheek, sucking it deliberately, and then rubbed me again with the wet paper. Her saliva made her thumb slippery, and it glided across my dick's shaft. I clenched my teeth and turned side to side, clutching my covers. She gained a lot in a short period.

Diana was sucking my cock, making her thumb wet now and then to keep torturing me that way, almost getting me to cumming before backing off. She refused to make me cum. She stopped as I got close to my orgasm, and as amazing as it sounded, I was getting irritated. "Are you going to make me cum or just tease me all day, honey?" I pleaded.

"I'm tempted to taunt you for an hour or two, but playing with you has made me fucking horny." She rose to her knees and hopped aboard my throbbing cock, thrusting down quickly. I went for Diana's breasts, bouncing with her thrusts, and thumbed her thick nipples, causing her to moan. I was so excited at that point that I couldn't stand it any longer, but I had to continue to hang on as much as I could for Diana's sake. But I didn't have long.

"I'm almost there, honey. Like, near..."
"Then it's sperm, boy. Don't be concerned for me. It's all cum inside me."
I let loose a torrent of sperm, drenching her pussy in ropes of hot, creamy cum. Diana rubbed her clit hard and heavy, and then she entered me, shutting her eyes and grunting as her pussy clenched my tired cock. She jumped on top of me, and we kissed passionately, our tongues touching each other's mouths as though it were our first heated embrace. There was never something dull about our embraces. Whether short or wild and passionate, our kisses were often full of affection and desire for each other.

We lay on my bed; two fulfilled, content, and caring people. Kissing, caressing, and touching, "I love you very much," I said quietly, my fingertips teasing the back of her hair.

"I adore you as well. What's the one thing I'm looking forward to about our prom? We spent nearly the whole night together. Maybe not going home until the following morning."

"Diana, that sounds wonderful, but I'm not sure what my parents will do. I'm not sure how to approach them about it. Can you honestly believe your parents would be okay with you coming home at 11 a.m.? In your prom gown?"

"Not in my uniform, with my neighbors watching. But I, and you should carry a change of clothes. We remain in a hotel and sleep together after that. "With a slight chuckle, she said. "Seriously, as long as I don't flaunt it, my parents would be perfect."

"Maybe you should speak to my parents about it because I'm not sure how they'll respond. Keep in mind that I have a younger sibling. I doubt they'll like the message that brings to Camilla."

"Oh, no. That didn't occur to me. In an ideal future, it wouldn't matter if it was your sister or one of my brothers."

"Please let me know when we've arrived at the perfect universe. You could be the only girl whose parents will allow her to come home late in the morning. Please allow me some time to focus on them. I guarantee I'll try. That's something I'd be interested in as well. And if it doesn't work out, we'll have opportunities to spend evenings together by the autumn. And, in the fall, we'll all be gone together. There are numerous possibilities there."

"I understand. Still, I need you right now, hugging me all night." We embraced and cuddled. We needed to pick it up. However, we had time. The phone then rang, and I was forced to answer it in my bed.

"What's up? Grossman's house."

"Hello, Jon," said a cheerful man. The voice was familiar to me. Adrienne, my mate, had called. Since I can recall, our families have been acquaintances since they became our next-door neighbors, and Adrienne and I grew up together before they relocated to Westchester when she was ten years old. Our families were acquaintances, and we saw them three or four times a year, and Adrienne, or Ade as I named her, and I became friends in our own right. Nothing more, but we would get together on our own a couple of times, particularly on New Year's Eve when neither of us had a date. As mates, of course. I hadn't mentioned Diana to her.

"Hello, Ade. It's great to hear from you. But it's not the right moment for me. Is it possible for me to contact you at 9 p.m. tonight? I've got a number to catch you up with."

"Sure thing, Jon. That will suffice. So I'd like to ask you for a comment. Will you accompany me to my prom? I don't have a deadline, and it's the week after yours."

With Diana right there, I felt uneasy. "I'll speak to you about it later tonight. I'll speak with you later, hun." I could sense Diana's gaze burning through me as we hung up the call. "Ade?" she inquired simply. But not so quickly.

"That's Adrienne, my dear. We met through our relatives, much like you and Steven. I've known her since I was a kid. We've been more than just colleagues. We've been out a few times, but only with Dutch friends, and mostly only as companions. Never again as someone else."

"So, how come you didn't tell me about her? Remember what I said about Steven?" Her eyes were filled with anguish. She was right. I should've told Diana about Adrienne a long time ago.

"Sincerity? I'm not sure. She was never a date; we kissed as friends would, except though we went out for New Year's Eve this year. But you're right. I could have mentioned her to you." I continued to tell her everything I knew about Adrienne. Then I told her. Ade invited me to accompany her to her prom, which was the week after ours.

"So, what do you think? What would you say to her? Can you accept her or not?" I was in the kennel here.

"That is all up to you, honey. I'm trying to assure you that you have nothing to be jealous of, but if you are, it's my fault. I want her to be willing to go somewhere with others, but I won't do that unless you don't get injured. If it bothers you in some way, I'll tell her no. You come first, regardless of how long she's been, my mate. You will still be first."

We were nude on the side of my bunk, and Diana was covered up with a portion of my scarf. She felt embarrassed that I had hurt her by not asking her anything she had a right to hear. Her tears streamed down her face.

I put my arm around her waist, and she didn't want to back away, but she also didn't get closer to me. "Diana, my darling, I will do everything in my power to make things right between us. All go."

"Please tell me something. Is she attractive?"

Weep. "She is, without a doubt, stunning. Yet, I'm not drawn to her. She's more like a sibling to me."

"Do you have a photo I should look at?"

"Of course, give me a second." I rummaged in the lower drawer of my nightstand, where I store my mementos, including Diana's panties that she had sent me. I went through a stack of photos and came upon a few with Adrienne in them. I handed them over to Diana, pointing out Adrienne in a party shot from her Sweet Sixteen two years earlier. She seemed more mature now, as did we all; however, you could say she was a beauty. Her red hair flowed down below her ears, and she had lovely blue eyes: a lovely face and a curvy figure. For the umpteenth time, I asked if she was unattached.

"She's beautiful. It doesn't make it any simpler for me to say, okay, go ahead."

"Diana, do you believe I would remain loyal to you? Consider it for a moment before responding."

"Jon, I don't have to worry about it. I have confidence in you. But should I put my faith in her? That is the crucial issue."

"Even though you had a good cause to be concerned, you know I would never cheat on you. Never, ever. I've got an idea. Why don't I see if she's available next Sunday and we can travel up to White Plains to visit her? She is still unaware of your existence. I haven't talked to her since we began dating. My whole focus has been on you." Diana allowed me to draw her near, and I kissed her head, then her lips. "I want her to be my mate, but you have to be safe for that to happen."

"OK, ask her when you speak later today. And what about Jon? There will be no more such mysteries. If there's someone else I might know about, I need to know right away."

"There are no female mates like that. We have an old male mate, but we aren't near. Douglas is a man with many talents. Syosset, New York. I see him when our parents get together, and even then, not all the time. There is no one else for you to be concerned with."

"Okay, fine. One query, Jon: where is she going to college?"

"There's no need to worry about that too. She'll be attending the University of California, Irvine. She wishes to move to Southern California. I'm not sure why." Diana grinned, and we felt much happier. Most of the time. Stuff will be fine because she knew Adrienne. There was little to be concerned for.

We got washed up and dressed, got something to drink, and Diana left after around a dozen farewell kisses. Before Camilla arrived home, I took a hot shower and changed into clean clothes. My parents arrived home first, before 6, followed by my mum. She dashed upstairs to her room to change, and after fixing her hair in the bathroom we shared, she was happy to accompany me to dinner. Despite my objections, Dad gave me $20, and Cammy and I went to Tong Fung, our family's Chinese restaurant a short 5 minutes south. A nice family-friendly restaurant with decent service.

Camilla was beaming when we were seated. We hadn't done this in months, going out for dinner with the two of us. We spoke after we ordered. I figured she was concerned about my leaving for school in the fall, and we thought about it, even though we had done so briefly the week before. This was a more in-depth debate. I assured her that I will still be available to her, even if only by text. She was concerned with moving to college because it was her turn if our mother wasn't doing well. I informed her that if she decided to leave when the time came, I'd stay close to home if necessary so she could go anywhere she wanted. "Cammy, that's just reasonable. And you know I'm going to miss you when I go, so stay in contact and call me."

"With school and Diana, you won't have time for me." She wasn't unhappy, but she was solemn.

"Cammy, there will never be a day when I won't have time for you. I'm not sure what would happen to Diana and me. Maybe we'll get married one day; maybe we won't. Who knows? Yet you will always be my sister. You'll still be a part of my life, even in fifty years."

She laughed, and I believe she was relieved that I was leaving. Camilla realized I couldn't survive without her in my life.

When we got home, she kissed me on the cheek and went up to her room to do some schoolwork, so I dialed Diana's number. We had a nice long chat, and she had been feeling stronger since that afternoon. I had to go to contact Adrienne because it was almost 9 p.m. "Diana, my sweetheart, I adore you. Do you want me to contact you when I finish speaking with Adrienne?"

"If it is until 10 a.m. Tonight I'm a little tired. But no later than ten o'clock. We'll meet again in the morning. Do you want to pick me up?"

"You've had it, as always. Good night, honey, just in case."
"Good night, too, sexy one. And I adore you as well."
We hung up, and I dialed my friend's number. I informed her this after we exchanged pleasantries "I have to tell you something, Ade. I'm heading on a serious date with somebody. We are madly in lust with each other. And it turns out that we'll both be attending Binghamton this fall."

Adrienne was first deafeningly quiet, but then she spoke up, "Jon, I'm delighted for you. Extremely. Yet, a part of me always hoped we'd end up together. I wished you'd make a run at me a couple of times. Especially on New Year's Eve. When you didn't, I was so sad. Still, I could see why you didn't. We have a great friendship. It might have been strange."

Before I said something, it was my turn for silence. "Ade, I can't pretend I didn't consider it a few times during the last year. But I never expected to get a signal from you that you needed me to, and what if I did and you ignored me? It might have made things very complicated for us later on. And if we started anything and it didn't work out, we'd both lost a good friend."

"I understand. However, I believe I would have taken the chance."

"You are aware that you will be visiting California in a few months. What would have happened if it had happened?"

"I understand. There are several future issues. Nonetheless...tell me about Diana. How did you meet, and how did things get so serious between you? Platter" I told her the tale without getting into specifics. Ade and I were able to communicate freely and frankly. We always understood when the other had lost their virginity, and we were honest with our feelings about sex. She was aware of my past attempts with other ladies. Still, I needed to keep Diana's particulars secret. I cherished her so much to tell anybody about it unless there was a crisis. Adrienne may have been the first person I would have approached with a female viewpoint.

She asked a few questions, nothing too intimate, and she realized how intense my feelings for Diana had been. "I'm delighted for you, Jon. I am overjoyed. I'm not going to get too close to anyone right now. As you said, I'll be in California in August. That's why I don't have a prom date. Have you considered becoming my escort?" She did not say the word "date."

"Ade, Diana answered the phone when you called, and like a jerk, I never told her about you. That stung her. It's entirely my responsibility."

"And it scares me as well, Jon. Didn't you tell her about me? We've been best friends since we were kids. And you've been seeing her for over a month without saying anything about me. With one deletion, you reach two goals."

No, no. Once more. I was very screwed up. In very separate cases, I wounded two women I cared for. I corrected one ailment. I had to repair the other. "How would you like to meet

Diana, Ade? If she met you, I don't think she'd mind if I went to your prom. In addition, I want my girlfriend and best friend to get to know each other. I'm sorry if I offended you both. I've made amends with Diana. I also want to make it right with you. Adrienne, will you please? I'm more upset than I can express."

She let out a breath. "We're mates too long for me to be angry at you for this, Jon. I'm always saddened, so I forgive you. And I'd just want to see her. When would you want to move up here?"

"I was dreaming about Sunday. We will just head out to lunch or dinner together."

"Arrive at 3 p.m. We'll head out to eat. And what about Jon? You're making a purchase."

I chuckled to myself. "Done and done. It's well worth the cost of stability. Anything less than a buck and ninety-nine cents." Adrienne burst out laughing. We'd figure it out. But we had a plan for Sunday. My two favorite women were going to be, in addition to my mother and sister. It should go off without a hitch. Is that correct?

That week was jam-packed. She was quite occupied. I still took a day off from work to devote some time to research. Diana and I practiced in the afternoons on Tuesdays (when I was off work) and Thursdays and all afternoon and evening on Monday. Except for a few embraces, we were mostly fine. She helped me get through a stumbling block of science by making me grasp a couple of ideas that were preventing me from progressing. Her mother welcomed me to return for dinner, allowing me to stay and complete further work. I had to operate on Wednesday, so Diana went shopping with her mother to dress for our prom. I had decided to get ready for a tuxedo after school on Monday. Diana was accompanying me.

Friday night was our date night, with no schoolwork and just fun together. We went to a tiny cafe with outdoor tables on Austin Street in Forest Hills, about 20 minutes from where we stayed in Bay Terrace, as the weather warmed up. My buddy Kevin and his partner Elyse were with us. They were a sweet pair, both chubby and full of energy. Diana got along well with them, and there was much fun.

It was unusually humid but completely relaxing. Diana wore a light white jumper over a black floral blouse and a pair of Calvin Klein jeans that suited her perfectly. At sunset, we ate and talked. After dinner, we went for a stroll down Queens Blvd., a 10-lane road lined with shops and restaurants for miles. We eventually got back in my car and drove to Irish Eyes, a bar, to go dancing. We danced for a few hours in another location with live music. My happiest moments were when the song was soft and sexy, and I could pull Diana tight as we danced to the beat. Her head leaned on my side, and her arms wrapped tightly around my back. Guys, like people, need to feel protected, and I felt safe in her arms. And, of course, I was aroused by her proximity to me. She changed her posture to expand our touch because she could sense my erect cock pushing between us.

"You're such a tease," I said quietly.

Diana grinned as she gazed up at me. "Take a look at who's spoken. You want me, but the only place we can spend tonight together is in your vehicle. We just ought to come up with a solution. I enjoy being willing to stretch out on a bed with you. The car runs, but it's cramped inside."

"So, what do you think? Tight is preferable. "I sent her a somewhat lecherous grin.

"The pervert. That's a positive thing I like about you. I enjoy being with you, but it's not private in your vehicle, sweetheart. I'm not sure what we should do with it. So the more we've been married, the more I want to be with you like every other partner. It doesn't have to be a bed...there are other rooms where we can have a ton of fun...but we need privacy."

When the music finished, we congratulated the band and then waited for a bit before the next song began. Kevin and Elyse joined us, and we ordered a round of beers. We spoke for a bit, but it was clear that they needed to be alone like Diana and me. And they had a destination in mind: Elyse's basement. They'd have plenty of privacy down there if they were discreet as they came in. That's fantastic.

We told them that we would take them there. Elyse said, "If you two need a place to stay, there's a huge basement. It won't be private, but neither will we be on top of each other." Diana and I exchanged glances, and I saw Kevin laughing softly from the corner of my eye. He was hoping we might say yes.

As I looked at Diana, we were both at the stage to communicate through our eyes. This was something we all agreed on. "Thank you, just no thank you. We'll skip it. "Kevin was disappointed when I mentioned this. I'd have to reconsider my friendship with someone who wanted to witness my girlfriend and me having sex. I believe he was hoping for something else than to look.

We drove away after dropping Elyse and Kevin off at her place. We remained silent for a few moments, not saying something. "Pull over, Jon, please," Diana said. It was so nice of her to be so respectful all the time, much like me.

I found a parking space and shut off the engine. This wasn't a sex stop since we were on a path with houses on all sides. "All right, honey. Please tell me what's going through your head. I know what Elyse said irritated you. It bothered me as well."

"I understand. I could tell from the look of your eyes." She shifted in her place, turned to face me, and said, "Could you please catch me for a moment? I need your help."

"Without a doubt. You're welcome at any moment, honey." I shuffled alongside her, and Diana stepped the rest of the way to me, into my arms, and let me cover her in my embrace. She was sobbing quietly, and all I could do was hold her until she settled down a little. "Diana, would you think I might have agreed to what they suggested? Is that what's bothering you?"

"No, I didn't want you to. I believe. I'm not sure. Damn, all of this is still too fresh to me! I had a bad feeling about you for a split second before you grinned at me. Then I realized you wouldn't. That's not correct. I was aware of it previously. Still, I had a little question. And I'm kicking myself for not trusting you absolutely because I should have known better."

I felt a surge of affection rush through me as I stroked her long brown hair, smooth and fine. Diana's minor insecurities helped me admire her even more. "I adore you, honey. I will never really consider doing anything like that. And I'm pretty sure I'm through with Kevin as a buddy. The look he gave me when Elyse said that. You're treated as though you're a slice of meat to be shared. I'm positive he tried to screw you. Like in a swap. As if I'd do that to you. Never, ever, ever in a million years."

"I understand. Like I previously said, I am always discovering how to fall in love with another."

"The same thing happened to me. This is a different section for me. In several cases, it's the most difficult aspect. But have a peek at it tonight. We were able to communicate with each other without saying anything. It wasn't a tough subject to explore. Yet, we got the job done. We have faith in one another."
Diana drew closer to me, creating quiet, contented noises. As much as I wanted her before, this was an incredible feeling. I was willing to remain in that state before it was time to go home. Diana, on the other hand, had other plans. And I didn't mind a bit.
"Let's go be alone, Jon. I want to love you as much as you want to love me."
"Pleased to meet you, honey. I adore you." So we went to that tiny and secluded secret spot I imagined as ours. However, on that warm Spring night, there were already three cars parked there, which was the maximum number allowed.

Diana replied, "Shit," a single term that best described our condition. We were barred from entering. I tried to come up with an alternative but couldn't come up with something. Diana's features brightened. "I've got an idea. It's a bit dangerous, but I believe we'll be fine. I doubt anybody else would show up."

"Is it risky? My crazy, sweet love. Tell me where you're going. We'll know how dangerous it is. Or it might be risky, "I teased her, and then I kissed her. She was still grinning. That alone made me feel a whole lot stronger.

"A little bit of both. The football stadium. Under the night sky."

Our high school practiced on a football field about a half-mile away from the school. It was fenced in, but there were gaps if you looked hard enough. "It sounds lovely, honey. Let's get started. In case we get cold, we'll have a towel."

"I doubt we'll get the chance to get cold," Diana joked, and I chuckled along with her. It wasn't a huge joke, but when you're madly in love with someone, something will make you laugh.

I stopped across the street in front of a private building, and after I got my blanket, we silently closed the car doors and then the trunk. We crossed the quiet street and didn't have to look long to locate a crack in the barrier. We moved together to the 50-yard line. It seemed to be acceptable.

We spread out the (thankfully) dark-colored blanket and sat in the middle. We were hugging and embracing within seconds. Our bodies brushed together in a manner that was both delicate and urgent, with Diana encircling my upper leg and drawing me tighter to her. "It was an excellent plan, love. There's plenty of room, and it's a bright, clear night. And she's a really warm lady who I adore."

She kissed my neck, and I closed my eyes to savor her grace, fire, and affection. I was already tough, so I wasn't in a hurry, and Diana wasn't either. She assisted me in removing my red IZOD shirt and kissed me all over my chest before teasing my nipples with her tongue. It wasn't as hard as it might have been for a woman (from what I could tell), but it felt pretty darn fine. I undid her blouse and yanked her arms loose.

"Keep an eye on me," Diana said, pulling me back a bit. "Sweetheart, lie down on your stomach." She knelt above me, behind me, then reached out carefully to unhook her bare bra. She eased it down her arms slowly, taking her time. As the bra fell off her body and showed me her breasts, her grin was provocative and attractive. I took a few deep breaths. Seeing

Diana nude or partially naked still had an impact on me. I reached out to stroke her, but Diana resisted and said, "No, not yet, lover. Only keep an eye on things."

She stood up, rapidly glanced around to make sure we were alone, then pulled off her jeans and stood over me in only her panties, another pair she had purchased the day before. These were purple, mostly see-through in the front and back (she turned to show me), and had a black satin panel concealed her cunt. There was enough ambient light from the half-moon and surrounding streetlights for me to see her, and what I saw made me want her almost as bad as when she was wearing stockings and a garter belt. Those were my favorite kinds of outfits. They were extremely enticing. Diana's voice and temperament, though, became the true seducers. Her self-assurance about her sexuality was breathtaking.

Diana said as she knelt back down on the blanket, next to me, before I could kiss or even stroke her, "Now it's your turn, sexy one. Get up and make a little fun of me." Her expression was covered with a sly grin.

There was a small chance of being noticed by those walking by on the street beyond the gate, which was part of the excitement. Besides, it was a little dangerous at the time, and Diana desired it. Without tearing my gaze away from hers, I stood up and steadily undid my belt, then touched my bulge through my tan jeans. It was so dark outside that I could hear her heavy breathing. I unbuttoned the waistband button and slowly drew my zipper back. "Does this appeal to you, baby?" I said it in the most seductive tone I could muster.

"You know I do," Diana said, staring at me as though I were her prey. Her right hand was in her pantyhose, and her left was adjusting her right breast. "But don't give up. I'd like to see something."

I knelt to remove my socks, but I wore white underwear that almost glowed in the silence. Anyone walking or driving by will see any asshole standing on the 50-yard line in his panties. Diana burst out laughing as I rapidly fell to the bottom, realizing my 'issue.'

"Yes, it's very amusing. You want us to be apprehended?" I said this while gently licking her all over her forehead.

"No way, no how. Still, you dropped to the ground as if the world had been yanked from under your foot. It was amusing. "She continued to giggle.

"You're now smiling at me. How will a man work while his girlfriend is laughing at him?" I appeared to be upset. I wasn't particularly successful at it.

"Is my big heavy wrestler angry because of his petite girlfriend?" Diana teased me as she wrapped her arms around my waist.

"Maybe a little bit." I slipped my arm under her hip and across her back, tightening her grip. Her nipples were firm, and that wasn't because of the cold breeze.

"So allow me to make amends to you, sexy man." A long embrace exploded in all of our bodies and hearts, and my hands went further down to grab her butt softly and with blazing passion. I rolled on top of Diana, she forced my briefs down just over my butt, releasing my erect dick, and I yanked her panties to the side. She drew her legs back, allowing me to slip my cock into her cramped and dripping house. As the top side of my cock rolled over her clit, it felt like we were sinking into molten gasoline, and we both gasped. "That's fantastic, sweetheart. You make me feel nice." As I tipped my head back, she kissed my throat, and I cried quietly.

"Just as you do to me, honey. So, so fine." We were moving in sync, seeking our pace as always, my hips rising and dropping as Diana locked her legs behind my thighs. My legs widened to give me more strength, as I'd seen in boxing, but this wasn't a battle. It was a lover's party, the most romantic thing two people might share. As we eased together into an emotional climax, I was overcome with passion and began singing in Diana's right ear Jackie Wilson's "To Be Loved," a sexy, soulful love song. When I finished performing, I kissed her ear and throat, and we went faster, my thrusts becoming faster and her hips moving to accommodate me. We were soon traveling at a quicker pace, on the same route, and when I arrived, it was like a torrent bursting inside Diana's cunt, which spasmed around my dick, raising my enjoyment. Diana let me go when every drop of me had been drained from my balls, and I rolled to her side, where she turned with me.

"You didn't cum, love," I said, my face flushed and drenched with sweat.

"No, but it all felt great. I adore you, my dear. That tune... I had no idea you could sing so good." Her loving hand stroked my jaw, but her eyes were more curious.

I was ashamed, but I felt compelled to justify. "Yes, most people think I can sing well, usually Blue-Eyed Soul, but I can't sing in public. I feel like I'm about to seize up. I was never able to participate in the school musical. I'd almost definitely be asked to play one of the leads if I tried out, and I really can't succeed in front of a crowd. Singing for you alone is difficult for me. It just kind of came out of nowhere."

"It's a lovely tune, and you performed it beautifully, but it sort of overwhelmed me because I wasn't expecting it at all. It was lovely, Jon. You are welcome to perform for me at any time. I hope I could sing just as well as she does. I may sing a melody, but that's about it. I'm weeping just thinking of you, Jon." Her eyes were wet, just not from sorrow. I kissed her on the cheek.

"I apologize for ruining your orgasm, love."

"Don't be one. I can have an orgasm at any moment, particularly while you're around." She grinned wryly, her eyes welling up with tears. "But learning that my boyfriend can sing like that is incredible. I'm hoping you won't give up performing for me. It will be heartbreaking for me."

"I'll do anything for you. For every moment. Diana, do you need me to make you cum before we leave?"

"No, I'm fine, sweetheart. I'm stronger than average. Besides, we need to get moving. You have jobs tomorrow, and we're hoping for the best here." We kissed again and hurriedly packed. After passing through the gate, we folded the blanket and returned to the vehicle. Diana replied, "Thank you, darling," as I warmed up the engine.

"You never have to praise me for loving you or revealing that to you, honey."

"No way, no how. I stared up at you as you were on top of me, making love to me, and there were all these stars all over your head. It was stunning, one of the most stunning items I've ever done. And I have a gorgeous boyfriend in the world. Who now sings to me as well. I really can't believe I waited too long to learn that for you."

"Diana, I'm not particularly attractive. Women are stunning. Men are attractive. At least some of them are."

"You're mistaken, sweetheart. Because of who you are, you are stunning. Yes, I think you're attractive as well. Extremely. I'm attracted to you just by staring at you. But you're stunning on the inside."

The moon shone through the window on Diana's forehead, and I thought to myself, not for the first time, how fortunate I was to have met her. It was more than just a sexual desire, which is how most partnerships begin. If we're fortunate, we'll discover something far richer to cultivate and flourish alongside one another. I don't mind if I sound mushy or less than a man,' whatever that is. Everything I thought about at the time was finding the genuinely unique person to develop with.

I couldn't answer orally because I was too choked up. I couldn't open my mouth without letting out a tiny sob from deep inside. Diana didn't need me to say anything; she just pressed my head against her chest and let me cry. She realized there was no pain there, just a lot of passion. Her fingertips ran into my hair and down the back of my neck. It looked almost as amazing as having sexual relations with her. I finally pulled myself together and kissed her several times until we both hugged each other. I glanced at my watch and noticed that it was almost 2 p.m. and that I needed to send her home. I wanted to get some sleep because I had to be at work at 9 a.m.

Our kisses goodnight was rushed. "Honey, I adore you very much. I despise needing to hurry through this portion of our evening."

"So do I, but you can get some rest. When can you get home from work? I believe my parents are leaving, and I will be able to get rid of Walt and Will for a few hours. If not, we should simply hang out."

"Either way, it sounds amazing to me. Goodnight, sweetheart. I adore you."

"Good night, everybody. I adore you as well." She was inside, behind the fence, after one more embrace. I returned home and went to bed, reflecting on how fortunate I was once more.

XXXXXXXXXXXXXXXXXXXXXXXXXXXXXXXXXXXXXXXXXX
XXXXXXXXXXXXXXXXXXXXXXXXXXXXXXXXXXXXXXXXXX
XXXXXXXXXXXXXXXXX

I got through work tiredly, which had been a Saturday ritual. But it was worth it on Friday evenings. As I called Diana, I learned that her parents were leaving. The poor news was that Walt and Will weren't there. But we were going to spend the night at home watching a movie. It was fine; I was sleepy, so a peaceful evening sounded appealing.

We brought in a pizza for the four of us to eat, and after a slight debate over which movie to see (which Diana and I won, of course), the twins grew relaxed lying on their stomachs on the concrete, while Diana and I sat behind them on the sofa. We put on Young Frankenstein, and everybody, including Walt and Will, was laughing before Diana and I began kissing. Then we weren't laughing when it was necessary. We were so preoccupied with being preoccupied.

"Hey, that's our sister back there," one of the twins exclaimed without looking at us.

"Yes, indeed! We'll beat you if you don't take your hands off. Two players against one!" I didn't know which was which, but I did know that even though I was a wrestler, there were two of them, both bigger than me, albeit a little thinner. Of course, it was just a prank, and Diana and I both chuckled hysterically, but it was strange making out with her when her brothers were aware of what was going on.

The Producers, led by Mel Brooks, was my comedy favorite after Young Frankenstein. However, the original 1968 production starring Gene Wilder and Zero Mostel was not the film adaptation of the musical. Nobody else had seen it, and after ten minutes, we were both laughing so much that they figured it was the funniest movie ever. I felt the same way.

It was a pleasant evening; I got to know Diana's brothers better and got along well. They were nice men, big and attractive, and may have been smarter than their genius sister. I left early because I wanted to get a good night's sleep, and we were heading up to Westchester to see Diana and Adrienne the next day.

So, after a decent night's sleep, I awoke at 8, got some workout (I had my last wrestling match of the year, and hopefully of my life, coming up on Thursday), and spent the morning doing research. I was getting behind in my studies due to work and Diana. I didn't know much, so I wasn't a genius like Diana. She needed to work, so I needed to work much harder. That morning, I accomplished a lot.

About the fact that we weren't supposed to be at Adrienne's before 3 p.m., I picked Diana up at noon to go out to lunch and enjoy some time together. We went out to lunch, which was her treat, and then we had an hour to spare. We exchanged a kiss while smiling at each other. For an hour, we realized just where we were going. Our secret place. It was secluded, but even if it were bright outside, we'd have plenty of anonymity if no one else was there.

We were blessed with good fortune. There was no one else around when I put the car in park, turned off the ignition, and within 3 seconds, we were kissing like two sex maniacs. We were pretty much, at least in terms of our relationship. We were moving as though we hadn't had sex in weeks, not two days— currently, less. We desired and needed one another. When we got to the back, I undid Diana's pantyhose, leaving her short skirt alone and even her jacket on. We didn't have much time, and we didn't want to look sloppy. "Just go down on me, sweetheart. I'd like to see your tongue on my vagina. After that,

I'll do the same for you. You haven't fed me in a week. "She said this with a hungry pout. Diana pouted beautifully.

"You don't need to remind me yet. I'd love to have my hands on your pussy." I positioned myself between her bare legs and her now exposed cunt. Even though we were low in time, I always decided to taunt her first, and Diana did as well. So I kissed her thighs first, licking from the inside to the outside, by her delicate cheeks, and then the other leg, inside and bottom again, her most vulnerable regions. Diana grasped my head and raised her hips, attempting to entice me to begin devouring her dripping cream. Her skirt was wrapped around her waist, and we had a little towel under her butt to collect any juices I lost.

"Jon, as much as I enjoy your tormenting me, you'd best get back to work. Unless you don't mind if we don't have enough time for me to blast you." As I looked up, I saw a naughty, playful twinkle in her smile.

"Please accept my apologies, ma'am. I'll get to it right away." I spoke as though I were a simple-minded employee assisting his employer. My tongue and lips began to travel through her lips and folds.

"Ooh, I hope I like that demeanor...

OH Fuck, Jon, that's sooooo good...manly attitude. Good and helpful." When my tongue flickered up and down her juicy slit, she giggled between moans. My thumbs drew her lips apart so I could insert my tongue through her crack, as though I were attempting to fuck her with it. My lower lips mashed against hers while my tongue pushed as quickly as it could. Diana kept thrusting her clit up to my lips, so I took her clit between two fingers and lightly rolled it back and forth. "FUCK JONDON'TSTOPDON'TSTOPDON'TSTOPDON'TSTOPDON'TS TOPDON'TSTOPDON'TSTOPDON'TSTOPDON'TSTOPDON

Her hips twisted frantically beneath my mouth, she yelled. I kept driving as far as I could, not stopping until she ordered me to, a few minutes later, softly pulling on my side. "You're going to murder me one of these days," Diana exclaimed tiredly. "However, what a way to ride."

"Then I'd best figure out when to leave. I don't want to miss you over anything as insignificant as an orgasm, "I said while looking at her.

"Is it petty? You're crazy, aren't you? Those are the incredible orgasms. You're a hottie, dude." She struggled to sit up before I extended my hand to assist her, during which I received a series of wonderful kisses. "Seriously, my darling, I adore you. Not there about the orgasms. They are, though, a really good excuse." We embraced, and I could already sense her wafting up from her origins even though her perfume was permeating the air in my vehicle. It made me feel dizzy in a good way. Not to mention hornier than I had previously been.

"Thank you so much, my darling. It was a pleasure to do with you. I enjoy making you feel fine, particularly after the previous night's deprivation."

"Yeah, it had to have been piling up since then until you let it all out. You might tell you unlocked the floodgates." We both laughed as we continued to hug each other. Then I felt her hand cup my cock in my slacks, and I twitched as a result of her presence. "Now that you've had yours, it's time for me to get mine. So spread out around the seat and let me take control of your delectable dick."

We both pushed my jeans and shorts off, off one knee, and I swung my legs up onto the long bench seat. Diana slid her knees between my thighs and pulled my top up a little so she could lick my tummy all over. The touch alone made me gasp, and the flesh there trembled with enthusiasm. She kissed me at the base of my cock, where my balls meet my penis. Kisses up the shaft, to the head, then all over the head. Her tongue slithered out to taunt my head, and it was my turn to raise my hips off the seat unconsciously. My body was attempting to drive my cock deeper into Diana's mouth, and she was welcoming it, allowing me to slip over her tongue to the back of her mouth. When I went because far (not because I'm huge), she normally gagged a bit, but this time she didn't. I could see and feel her throat muscles adjusting to enable her to rub the head.

"Oh my goodness! I can't believe you're torturing me like this! It looks fantastic! My naughty, sexy baby!" She glanced up at me, but she didn't let go of my cock for a second. Her fingertips teased my balls as she bobbed up and down, picking up momentum, faster and faster, swallowing my cock as though she'd been doing it for years rather than only a few months. There were just so many I could bear until Diana took me back to her throat and choked while I blew my nut down her throat. Not a single decline, not even a smidgeononononononononononononononononononononon ononon. She took a step back, leaving me in her mouth until she was certain I was empty. I stared at her in awe; it was one of the best feelings I'd ever had in my life. Diana was also responsible for most of the other wonderful events. But this was a complete surprise.

As she let me go, I stood up quickly and kissed Diana as though I was still fired up. "Why did you pick up on that so quickly?" "Have you practiced with someone else?" I made a joke. I figured it wasn't the case, so I was intrigued.

"Wow, I have hundreds of guys lined up for blowjobs." "It was only a question of repetition," Diana said, a smart-ass smile on her face. "I just needed to do that. I was adamant. So I considered it and practiced calming my throat muscles, and when the time came, I went for it. It was much simpler than I had expected. I enjoyed seeing your response as it occurred. That look of delight and surprise. It was well worth the effort. It's a shame I won't be around to see it again. It will never be unfamiliar to you again."

"However, I'll be grateful." You're the most wonderful lady I've ever seen." Before we pulled ourselves together, we kissed a lot. We cleaned ourselves up with the towel, Diana placed her panties back on (boo! ), we all got out and straightened our clothing and hair, Diana tested her lipstick, and we were on our way to White Plains, an hour north.

We arrived at Adrienne's a few minutes late, but she was waiting for us at the entrance. We exchanged hello kisses and hugs, and I introduced the ladies to one another. All went swimmingly. We sat and spoke while drinking something, and Diana and Ade discovered they had stuff in common. Mostly, they're picking on me. It was what I should have predicted. But it was good fun. And it was wonderful to see how much they got together. It was also a little of a relief.

We got into the car around 6 p.m. to head to dinner. Adrienne sat in the front seat with me out of habit, not noticing it was now Diana's seat. It was uncomfortable, so Ade apologized and jumped in the back. She pointed me in the direction of a local Greek restaurant. When I was driving, and we were all chatting, Ade looked down to the floor of the car and asked, "What's this?" and I understood before she or Diana did.

"Leave it to go, Ade!" Too late, I yelled.

"Oh YUCK!" she exclaimed. That was the towel we had used to clean ourselves only a few hours ago. Diana turned white and sank into her seat.

"You didn't put it in the trunk?" she said, her teeth clenched.

"I hope not," I said, ashamed beyond words. "I'll pull over to get rid of that, Ade."

"How come you two fucked back here before coming to see me?" What the hell is going on, Jon? Then you're going to make me wait here? "Eww!"

I pulled over as fast as I could, got out, and grabbed the towel, which I tossed in the trunk. So much for my dreams to become acquainted with my partner and childhood pal.

When I got back in the vehicle, Ade yelled angrily, "Just drive me home." "I'm getting tired of eating."

"I'm sorry, Adrienne," Diana said before I could reply. We messed up. Believe me; I'm almost as embarrassed as Jon. We didn't plan for you to be aware of anything so private."

"Wow, you messed up, if you know what I mean." I can't believe I'm sitting here! It's fucking disgusting! I'm not angry with you, Diana, but you, Jon...how could you have placed me in this position? "After I told you how I felt last week," she added, sobbing. "What I want is to go married." And don't be concerned about my prom. Even if you asked, I wouldn't go with you now!"

"Come on, Ade..."

"Please don't Ade me!" "Don't bother talking to me!" As I arrived at her door, she fled inside, sobbing. As embarrassed as I was as Diana was, Ade was devastated on the inside. She kept out some expectation that things would somehow work out between her and me, despite the fact being. Still, there was no way, and that had nothing to do with Diana and I getting intercourse and leaving the evidence behind, nor did it have anything to do with the distance we'd be apart.

At that stage, neither Diana nor I were in the mood to feed. We didn't feel like chatting at all. The hour-long trip back to Queens seemed to last three. I figured that if Adrienne settled down, we'd be able to reach an agreement. But things weren't going to be that simple for her and Diana. Diana, being astute as she was, deduced that it was about more than a soiled towel. Regardless of what I thought, she was continuing to see Adrienne as a competitor. It had little to do with how I felt. She was aware of how women should be. Men are included as well. Adrienne will still be a source of contention for us.

"Honey, do you want to get anything to eat?" I asked as we crossed the Whitestone Bridge. "Can we talk about it?"

"Of course. We need to feed. Simply go to a cafe." Diana said it in a quiet sound, almost without emotion, as though she was filled with stone-cold rage. I pulled into a nearby diner's parking lot, and before we got out of the vehicle, she turned to me and said, "We should speak here first." Whether there's someone we recognize in there...

"All right, let's learn about it. I apologize for leaving the towel there, Diana. That was humiliating."

"Jon, her outburst may have begun with the towel, but her...rage... has nothing to do with the towel." She's got you on the phone. "Like, extremely."

"I understand." I sighed a rather dissatisfied note. "She's envious. She thought we'd wind up together somewhere. But she never mentioned anything to me or sent me any hints. And maybe that might have operated six months or a year earlier. But now I'm head over heels in love with you. Whatever Ade was dreaming or wishing about, it will not come true. And though she wasn't planning on moving to California. I've known her almost my whole life, and we've been best friends for the majority of it, and for the first time, I have no clue what she's thinking, apart from the obvious."

"Please accept my apologies, sweetheart. I believe she's had a crush on you for some time and is now unable to cope with the reality that she realizes it can't happen. It may, but it won't. "I think so." Diana felt insecure, and my heart ached for her. I slipped across the seat and encircled her, and she leaned her head on my back.

"That won't happen, honey. I've never been so serious before, but I'm not a liar. When I first began dating, I had a lengthy conversation with my father. He told me that many men play with their partners or wives behind their backs, but a true guy doesn't do that. If you're upset enough to consider adultery, you speak to your mate about it and attempt to hash it out. You, on the other hand, should not steal. Never, ever. I guess I'd be more concerned about disappointing him than offending you."

"Wait a minute. That's probably pretty cool. It makes me understand your spirit, Jon. And I had a feeling I liked your dad. You, too, mum. Still, I could say he was a good guy, and he is why you are a good man. Jon, it's fine if you plan to send Adrienne to her prom, even if she needs you to take her. I realize I can depend on you. It makes no difference what she wishes for. No, not to me. I don't want her to get hurt. A long as she knows ahead of time that you're not going to sleep with her. That's not what I'm doing, sweetheart. I understand how you do. I'm not going to instruct you how to deal with it."

"I'm not sure she needs me to take her. She is no longer interested in speaking with me. You're my greatest mate, honey. But Adrienne had been there for a long time. I'm going to be hurt if I lose her. As though I couldn't say you. But if I have to pick between you and everyone else, I'll go with you every time as long as we're together, whether it's a year, a dozen years, or a lifetime. In my core, you'll always be first. Yet, I pray to God that it worked out. I don't want to be without her." It was my turn to be angry and Diana's turn to console me.

"I don't want you to miss her. I want what you want, what makes you happy in every way. But if she's going to be on the phone with you..."

"I understand, honey. I'm not going to harm us like that. After my dad, you are the most significant individual in my life. No, the same as my family. I'm not going to harm you. "I'm afraid not." Diana cuddled up as tight as she could, almost inside my shell. I began singing 'Tupelo Honey by Van Morrison to her, and when I got to the first refrain, Diana just broke down, weeping in a good way. The evening had been very emotional, and the gentle and romantic song stirred up feelings that had been bubbling only under the surface for a previous couple of hours. We quickly find ourselves kissing passionately. But this was not the location for it. There are far too many customers arriving and leaving from the diner. However, there was a closed tire store next door, and the fence dividing the parking lots was still available for spillover parking whenever the diner was busy. It wasn't a busy Sunday night, so I pushed the car to the back of the tire store lot without really thinking about it. It wasn't the most romantic environment, but it was quiet and private. Besides, we were both so charged up; this wouldn't take long.

Diana was all over me before I could even get out of the vehicle. "Push the seatback," she advised, and when I did, we had enough room for what we wanted to do. She straddled my body and kissed me, her tongue exploring my lips. I had my hands on her panty-covered bottom, smooth and round, the panties protruding from the crack of her ass. When our mouths were locked together, my hands grasped her tightly. Her hands hurriedly opened my jeans and yanked my cock out from my panties. "Fuck you, Jon. Fuck me, don't make love to me!"

"Indeed, butter. "I'm dying to get inside your vagina!" Diana worked her pelvis around my cock and sat down hard after I yanked her pant crotch aside. We both screamed out as I looked at her, my face contorting with her intense desire rather than mine. As I kissed her neck and stomach, she was rubbing hard on my dick, her hips rolling in tight circles around my thighs. Diana drew her jumper up and drew her bra cups back. I assaulted her tiny, pale breasts greedily, not kissing her but sucking like a baby wanting milk.

"Bite them," she exclaimed, her eyes clenched and her hips pumping up and down on my sore cock. As my fingertips pressed deeply into her lips, I twitched inside her, and she grunted. I didn't bite down that hard, but she sensed it, and she charged at me as I'd never seen her before. The ferocity of her orgasm triggered mine, and I poured a colossal amount of cum inside her. Diana screamed again and returned, soaking my cock and my briefs. All smelled like Diana, even the vehicle and my groin, and it was the best perfume in the universe. I let her boobs go, and she bent her head down to kiss me repeatedly.

"That's incredible, honey. Simply incredible "With some challenge, I said.

"Oh, indeed. Baby, you've found the right expression." We kissed many times more. When I helped Diana adjust her bra and take her jumper off, our kisses were deeper. She arose from my withering dick, a dense strand of our fluids connecting us. "Where the hell is the damn towel when we need it?" We both burst out laughing. The towel was still in the wrong spot at the wrong moment.

She tightened her pantyhose before resuming her seat with such intensity that it felt as though she weighed a hundred pounds more than she did. I mocked her, "Really ladylike," and she slapped my shoulder.

"Coming from my wrestler boyfriend, of course. It sounds like clop clop clop all over the house as you move." We joked with each other as a group. Both the sex and the humor were rather cathartic, clearing our minds of a heavy load. "I don't think we should go in there and sit down, sweetheart. I'm scared to go home smelling like this. We stink of women."

"True? Take a look at my socks." My slacks' crotch had a distinct moist stain across the crotch. It even smelled of sex. "How am I going to get into my house? My parents will destroy me if Camilla is nearby."

"We'll both have to return home. Just hoping for the future. Alternatively, our parents could prohibit us from ever seeing each other again."

"That is just not going to happen. And if it means fleeing together." I was just half-joking. No one will be denied the opportunity to see the other; our parents were not like that. But even though they did, none would be able to hold us apart. "Are you at least hungry?"

"I'm hungry. Can we simply go to McDonald's? I will enter with less shame than you. My soiled clothes are covered. "She laughed. It was decided upon. Diana went into a nearby McDonald's to find us something to eat. Anything none of us ate regularly. Still, we had to do something because we were starving. We ate and spent time together in harmony and warmth. When we were over, I drove Diana home, even though it was still early, before ten o'clock. We were all mentally spent.

"Diana, thank you for being so patient. You can major in psychology. I think you'd be fantastic at it."

"You can also learn music. I'm all fuzzy inside because of the way you rap. And drenched." She gave a sexy grin. We kissed and hugged each other in front of her entrance, not wanting to let go, but it was necessary. We had to call it quits for the night. "Remember, we're going to get your tux tomorrow after practice."

"I understand, honey. I couldn't possibly forget. And my last match as a wrestler is on Thursday. You're coming to help me, right?"

"I wouldn't trade it for the world! It's true!" She kissed me many times. We heard her brothers reply, loudly, from the window next to the front door, "No, no! He touches her on the lips!" The ballbusters are the people that break balls.

We smiled, feeling less embarrassed than earlier in the day. Still, it was only one of those days. Diana had to go to her pain, and I had to go to mine. The mark on my jeans disappeared somewhat, though not significantly. And I always stank of sex. I was sitting in my seat, unsure about what to do, when I had an idea. It's not a brilliant plan, but it might succeed. I pulled over and got out, keeping the last of my soda in my cup. I braced myself for what was to come and spilled the remainder of the contents, Coke, and salt, into my jeans, almost gasped from the ice-cold substance reaching my crotch. Even though it was unpleasant, I was certain it would succeed. I got the infamous towel and dried off sufficiently to get back in my car and drive away. Sure enough, when I got home, the tale I said was verified.

My drink worked, and I was glad to get out of my jeans and other clothes and take a short shower.

After saying goodnight to my dad, I went to bed and talked about Diana and Adrienne. I wanted to wait a few days before contacting Ade to give her time to calm down, but not so long that she thought I had given up on her. Tuesday evening. That's when I'd dial her number.

XXXXXXXXXXXXXXXXXXXXXXXXXXXXXXXXXXXXXXXXXXXX
XXXXXXXXXXXXXXXXXXXXXXXXXXXXXXXXXXXXXXXXXXXX
XXXXXXXXXXXXXXXXXXXXXX

Diana and I headed to our nearest tuxedo shop after school on Monday. The owner had fitted my father and me for my Bar Mitzvah five years ago, as well as for a formal family wedding two years later. Milton, the owner, recognized me, if not by name, but I was impressed that he remembered anything at all. We all settled on a traditional black tuxedo with the ruffled cuffs and shirtfront that was fashionable at the time (what were we thinking?). Tie, cufflinks, black leather shoes... I was paying the same sum for a borrowed tux as Diana was for a dress she intended to keep. Aren't you nuts? But when the outfit was done, I looked fine. Diana was delighted. She said this after Milton was out of earshot "I wish I could take you behind the house and fuck you right now. That tuxedo. Ride you like a wild bronco and jump your bones! "With a soft chuckle, she said.

"You're aware of what you're doing to me, aren't you? I'll be more ashamed than I was yesterday if he has to weigh my groin again!"

"Do you suppose Milton would let us use a dressing room if we ask?" my she-devil asked, taking a short squeeze of my cock.

I pretended to pray to God by looking up at the ceiling. "Oh Lord, what have I made? Woman, thy name is evil!" I concluded by paraphrasing Hamlet.

Diana burst out laughing. "I'll keep that in mind the next time you're feeling horny. Which I unequivocally agree with." She took a little closer to me to whisper. "Is it true that your parents are at work? Is your sister already at home?"

"She shouldn't be there. She normally has her junior cheer squad meet on Mondays. She doesn't get home until about 5:30 p.m. Are you saying the same thing I am?"

"I'm thinking having my guy dressed like that has had me all worked up. You want to drive me home, then take me away?" Her eyes were brimming with mischief and fire.

"There's nothing I'd like to see more of." We exchanged a quick embrace until Milton brought out my rental agreement and my deposit receipt. I could pick it up two days before the prom and send it up to three days later without incurring late fees. This was going to be the most costly date of my life, along with prom passes, a tux rental, a corsage, and 'incidentals.' But it was well worth it to be there with Diana.

Diana and I had about an hour to be safe, so we went to my luckily quiet home. As I turned around to open my bedroom doors, she was already unbuttoning her blouse. Just not in a 'let's get into bed now' kind of way; she was staring me in the eyes and being cautious and careful, very seductive. One button at a time...slow and sexy...until it slipped off her shoulders. "Sexy dude, take a seat on the bunk. You're mine, fully mine ". She kissed my lips before continuing her impromptu strip tease after I sat down. She moved her fingertips gently along the edges of her black bra, tempting the heck out of me. Her fingertips

212

then went down her tummy as she sighed, a sexy echo. Diana then unbuttoned and unzipped her trousers. She turned around so I could see her back and rear, and she rolled her hips from side to side as she pulled her jeans off, revealing the matching black panties on the inside.

"Oh, boy, you're amazing!" I yelled as she shook her bottom to keep her jeans off. She got out and turned back, her head already bumping and grinding to music while she rubbed her hands through her hair. Diana, a child, no, a WOMAN, who had been so quiet on her own until only a few months ago, had layers upon layers of sexuality, the majority of which had yet to be uncovered.

"Do you agree? Play some songs. Anything enticing. Then get some money."

As a girl, it was like being let loose in a candy shop. I immediately went to my stereo and switched on a channel with some Latin dance music, and Diana quickly got into the groove. I then went to get my pocket, which had six singles. This was a fantastic fantasy, and not just for me.

Diana danced about, her hips and boobs swinging like a sex goddess, and I sat there, a missile rising in my lap. She was my sex goddess, and I was prepared to worship her. Diana placed her foot on my lap, not too forcefully because she didn't want to ruin the goods, and thrust her a$$ in my direction. I understood just what she desired. I tucked a dollar into her pantyhose band near her waist, then another near her right butt cheek. She kissed me, then turned and swayed a bit more; then I kept placing dollars in her panties while her bra fell off, and she rubbed her boobs in front of my face. Diana had them flapping around from her underwear as soon as I ran out of bucks. I was so hard that my cock hurt. Her nipples were tiny stones with a smidgeon of giving. Then she stepped up her game.

"You've been so kind, sir." She kissed me lightly, almost imperceptibly, like a real stripper would (I guessed). "We're not allowed to do anything, but...we have a spot for unique customers. Stuff happens down there that is out of the ordinary. Do you want to move into that bed, sir? "she said in a seductive, sultry tone. It exuded optimism, and I'm not sure where it came from.

I, on the other hand, was sweating internally, and it came out in my speech. In terms of imagination, I felt like I was with a true stripper/hooker. Everything I could say to her was, "Yes, please." Diana took my hand in a dainty, sexy way and helped me up, and of course, we were still in 'the space,' so our walk from one side of the bed to the other was extremely brief. It was amusing and amusing, and we all laughed briefly until she

214

perched on the edge of the bed with just her black panties. I sat down, but she prevented me by placing her hand on my stomach.

"Sir, I need to do an 'inspection,' if you know what I say. Anything, diseases, and everything." Oh, she was wonderful. Diana was living the part to the fullest. How did she even find out about these things? I saved the issue for later. It was now time to have some fun. "Can you kindly remove your trousers and shorts?" She had bright, playful eyes and a wide grin as she gazed up at me.

"I believe it would be more fitting if you let my trousers off. Your tip may be a reflection of your assistance." I looked at her like I imagined a 'john' would appear. That was whatever it was.

"The consumer is always correct," Diana said, opening my jeans and pulling them down my thighs, then taking my briefs off, so my hard dick bounced up to face her. "Hmmm, you seem to be clean." She was holding my dick, squeezing it this way and that, and checking it from any perspective. "There are no illnesses here. That's fine; we should get underway now. This isn't what I'm going to do. I'm going to be paying in advance, but because your pocket isn't easy for you right now... you seem trustworthy. Are you one of them?"

"Without a doubt. You can depend on me, Miss. I wouldn't rob you."

"Wow, I think you're going to stiff me nicely," Diana said as she licked all over the head of my dick, smiling up at me and smelling my tender meat.

"Oh, god," I moaned as Diana slipped her lips gently across my head as her tongue wet my dick. She went forward and then around, each time moving a little closer to the bottom. She was down on my cock and her nose in my pubic hair after only five occasions. My hands slid through her fur, grunting with delight at what she was doing to me. Diana's hands gripped my hips and squeezed, urging me to fuck her mouth, and I was all in. My hips were slowly pumping, and after a few strokes, she released me out of her mouth and just used her tongue. Then she sucked me again, and I felt my toes might fold into my heels. After a while, she gave my balls a tongue bath while her hand stroked me steadily but not quickly or hard enough to make me cum.

I adored this blowjob, but I still wanted to screw her. I reasoned that if she was going to play the part, we could go all the way. "I adore what you're doing to me, Miss. I've never seen a blowout like this before. So I just want to fuck you. Do you mind if I ask?"

"Not. Sucking your tasty dick has soaked my vagina, want to see?"

"Oh, indeed. I'd like to see how wet you are in front of me. Is it okay if I go see for myself?"

"Be my guest, girl," Diana said, leaning back on her elbows and spreading her legs wide. I knelt in front of her, and her smell struck me hard. That was the fragrance that set my heart on fire for her. By her hips, I grasped for the elastic of her pantyhose. "No, no, no. Simply push them aside, boy. I'd like you to fuck me when I'm wearing my panties. Will you help me with that?"

She was pushing one of my keys. I only nodded as my fingertips drew the crotch to the right, and her cunt was there for me, warm and moist and swollen. I bent in to lick her, but she grabbed my cheek. "There's no time for that baby. You'd better fuck me before the boss shows up."

Diana had a glazed expression on her lips, but her mind and body were full with me. "Get down to your feet. Please hurry. Just set aside your underwear for me."

Diana dashed over to prepare to be fucked doggy style. She was smoldering and more than ready. I was inside her vagina in two seconds because her fingertips kept the crotch apart. This was not about making love; it was about raw flesh.

I rolled about until I was completely inside her tight vagina, stirring up her juices with my throbbing dick. My groin was rubbing her curved, smooth bottom, which looked like paradise on my groin. Diana and I were both crying, and our bodies were joining as though we were one. "Fuck me! Come on, boy! Spank me as well! "she demanded vehemently, smacking her butt with a loud crack to emphasize her point.

"Do you like it a bit rough?" I grunted, not as her caring lover but as a guy there to take advantage of her.

"Yes, yes, yes! Pound my wet pussy right now!" Diana, my stunning, caring, and caring girlfriend, was a sexual wonderland. I began fucking her hard, the way she needed me to, and I was having as much fun as she was. I even put my hand on her butt, and it wasn't that tight. I'd never injured her. But clearly, it wasn't difficult enough. "I said spank me!" she exclaimed. She was fully immersed in the role of the sinful, wanton lady, and she was having a great time doing it.

We were fucking each other hard, thrusting into each other, and whispering nasty stuff to each other. I even pulled her hair for a while, and she never complained. She enjoyed it. I spanked her as much as I could stand it. Diana growled her way to a couple of orgasms until the major one. I reached around and rubbed her pussy and my balls while holding her tiny, pert boobs and teasing her nipples. This was the hottest, dirtiest thing we'd accomplished in our short time together, and it was incredible. Making love together was just as awesome but in a slightly different way. This was pure entertainment.

Whenever I moved into Diana, my pelvis slapped her butt, and hot, squishing noises came from her cunt. Her pussy was going quickly, and we were fucking strong. My body and head were leaking sweat onto her back. She pulled back hard and screamed out as she approached, her vice-like muscles squeezing my cock. I screamed almost silently as I soaked her walls with gobs of my sperm, my cock twitching at least four or five times before falling over on top of her back.

We lay there, radiant and glistening with sweat, totally engrossed in a natural high of passion. Diana giggled in a girlish manner that was the polar opposite of the lady she had appeared to be only a few minutes earlier when I kissed her shoulder and throat.
"MMMMMMMMMMMMMMMMMMMMMMMMMMMMMMM MMMMMMMMMMMMMMMMMMMMMMMMMMMMMM MMMMMMMMMMMMMMMMMMMMMMMMMMMMMM MMMMMMMMM

I rolled off of her, and she turned to lie on her back on my lap. I tickled her shoulder, and she tickled my tummy. It was incredibly sensual and soft. "Honey, I adore you. I'm not exactly where that came from, and I'm not sure I want to find out. I say I'm sure it's not something you've ever done for someone else. What I'm suggesting is that I don't want to look a gift horse in the mouth. I had a great time, as I do in anything we do together."

"I'll inform you. I'm not bothered." I instructed her to continue, and she did. "Last summer at camp, several of the female counselors were tossing around a collection of short stories focused on the adventures of a Las Vegas stripper. It was nonsense; it was a work of fiction. I'm fairly certain. Anyway, there was a tale in there that was almost exactly like what we did, and it made me very sticky. Of course, we all spoke about how disgusting, such reports were. We couldn't admit it made us hot. But it worked for me, and I'm sure it worked for a couple of people as well. All I know is that after reading that, I went into my bunk and masturbated as silently as I could. It was excruciatingly painful for me. You see how loud I am. But before I got inside, I had to hide my face in my sheet. I considered seducing this one guy I thought was cute, but I decided against it."

"Do you have any other thoughts based on those stories?" I inquired, curious as to what my sexy girlfriend's limit was.

"A couple," she teased, laughing. "We'll give a couple a shot. When we're alone with each other." And there were a couple of sweet kisses. "You should, after all, make suggestions. You can have everything you want. I guarantee that the least that might happen is that I say no. And there's not anything I'd refuse."

"I think I can do some reading," I said, smiling and kissing her. "When education is out. We both have a lot of reading to do for the time being."

We touched for a little while before realizing it was getting late. We needed to get washed up and ready, so I sent Diana to the bathroom while I straightened up my bunk, and then I sent her to get dressed while I went to the bathroom. I directed her to switch on the TV and wait downstairs as I dressed if my mother or Camilla arrived home. Cammy came home just when I was coming down the stairs, and when she saw Diana on the sofa, she went to her first to offer Diana a big hug. I was already formally second in my little sister's affections. So I did get a hug as well.

Mom arrived home ten minutes later, and I brought Diana home as she prepared dinner. Camilla insisted on accompanying us, and after attempting to dissuade her politely, I relented and joined us. Since my younger sister accompanied me, our farewell kiss will be short and less than enthusiastic. When I told Diana

I'd pick her up in the morning, she jumped out of the car way faster than I would have liked.

Camilla moved to the front, and when I pulled forward, she giggling and saying, "I'm sorry if I cramped your style, Jon," and I gave her a fake harsh smile, which made her giggle even louder.

"Yes, you most certainly are. I believe you would like to have a big sister rather than a big brother. "I pretended to pout when I said this.

"There is no way. I adore my older brother. But I wouldn't mind seeing a wonderful sister-in-law, "Camilla said, a wide smile on her face.

I gave her a look that said, "Are you out of your mind?" "Cammy, we're 18 years old, we haven't yet started college, let alone graduated from high school, and you're marrying me off? Are you going insane?"
"Wow, you love Diana, and you know it," Camilla said, absolute brat mode on.
"Yes, and I want to continue loving her. But I'm not quite set for marriage just yet."

"I know," my sister smiled, "so I want to be a bridesmaid!"

"And I promise you'll be a bridesmaid once I get married. And you'll have to wear an ugly gown, wear mascara, and get your hair styled in a fancy hairdo..."

"Is that true? Are you certain you don't want to marry Diana right now?" We all burst out laughing, a great hearty laugh.

"I'm fairly certain, pipsqueak." I arrived at our place. "Come on; dinner should be ready in a few minutes."

We went inside, and I could tell mom was worried about something right away. And it was aimed squarely at me. Mom kissed and hugged Camilla, but she gave me the cold shoulder. But whatever was troubling her had to do with me.

I couldn't work it out and assumed she'd let me know when she was finished. Dad arrived just after six o'clock, and we sat down for dinner at 6:30. Mom showed me the silent treatment, and no matter how much it bothered me, I wasn't going to question her what was wrong in front of Camilla. So dinner was a rather quiet affair, which was unusual for our household. Camilla and I washed up after dinner, putting things away and wiping down the counters as I heard mom and dad arguing in the living room, which was too low for us to notice.

Cammy said to me as we filled the dishwasher, "Mom's mad at you."

"The use of language. But, indeed. I'm not sure why. I'm certain I'll find out by the end of the night."

My father did indeed bang on my door when I was doing my homework, and Camilla was doing hers in her bed. "Can you please come downstairs, Jon? Your mother and I need to speak with you about something." It was phrased as a challenge, but it was more like an order from on high.

"Can you please give me two minutes? I'm working on a physics problem."

"As fast as possible. Make it fast." He went downstairs, and I was left scratching my head, trying to find out what the heck I had done. What I could think of were blanks.

I ended my dilemma and went downstairs to see what my parents were up to. Camilla's door was shut on my father's orders. This was a dangerous situation. I sat down and said, "So, what exactly did I do? I'm not sure."

Mom was the first to talk. "After you dropped Diana off, I went upstairs and passed by your bed, and your door was wide open.

The odor that emanated from your bed, Jon, was almost overpowering. I was aware of what you and Diana were up to. When you come downstairs, you should have closed the darn gates. If your sister had passed by and smelled it... I wouldn't have been able to have to smell it."

She was right. I was mistaken, and it's a good thing Cammy didn't go upstairs until we left. I didn't think to lock the door until I finished straightening out the bedding.

"I don't know what to think, Mom and Dad..."

Dad interrupted me. "We know you're both 18, and we know how it feels to be that age, particularly when you're in love. And if you're both away at college, you'll be free to do anything you want. But you're still here, and as long as you are, you'll respect your family, especially your mother and sister. We've offered you a lot of leeways, and we're guessing Diana's parents do as well. That is their concern. We're not thrilled that you took her here and had sex, so if you're going to do it, at the very least spray some air freshener or open a window afterward. And once your sister found out, you'll be suspended before at least college. Do you see what I mean?"

"Completely. I'm sorry, Mum. I pledge to be more polite. I'm not going to say Diana; I doubt she'll ever come here again, particularly now that you're here. "I addressed my mother directly. "This will never happen again."

"See why it doesn't," mom said as she stood up, already angry.

Dad said, "All will be fine. Your mother has to get over it. In the morning, she'll be perfect. Please keep in mind that there are other people in the building, including your younger sister. Certain aspects aren't essential for her to know just yet."

I went back and completed my homework before making myself scarce for the remainder of the evening. Sure enough, all was perfect with my mother the next morning, and I never discussed it with Diana. I tried calling Adrienne that night, but she didn't answer her phone and didn't return my post. I even called her house phone and left a message with her mother on Wednesday night, but I didn't get a callback. It was painful to see her avoid me, but there was nothing I could do about it.

My last wrestling match was on Thursday after training. Diana came to help me and also took Camilla with her. They both caused a lot of noise for me, but as I've said, I was a decent wrestler at best, and my competitor was a beast on a wrestling scholarship at a big Midwest university. I gave it my all, but he beat me 3 points to 1, and it wasn't even near. That was the last time I fought.

During the game, Diana and Cammy approached me to comfort me, one with a kiss on the cheek and a hug, the other with a couple of kisses on the mouth and a larger hug. "You shouldn't be kissing me at all, any of you. I badly need to take a shower."

"We figured you would need some help," my sweetheart of a sister said as I rubbed her scalp.

I knelt in front of her and said, "That's why you'll always be my sweetheart," and she smiled warmly.

Diana kissed me again and added, "And that's why you'll always be MY sweetheart," in her soft smile.

"Are you sure?" With a grin on my face, I inquired.

"Possibly. Who knows? You are correct; you do need a shower. I'll treat the three of us out to dinner after you clean up. Chinese food for me!"

XXXXXXXXXXXXXXXXXXXXXXXXXXXXXXXXXXXXXXXXXX
XXXXXXXXXXXXXXXXXXXXXXXXXXXXXXXXXXXXXXXXXX
XXXXXXXX

Our prom was three weeks away. I spent the afternoon having a trim and a professional shave with aftershave (ouch). When I got home, I changed into my tux and took a nice, hot shower. I spent an hour getting ready, making certain that I looked fine. I even made my mother do my bowtie, and she looked at me as if I were the best thing that had ever happened to her. I guess I was until Camilla came along.

"You're too handsome!" mom exclaimed after she was done inspecting me like an inspection. She kissed my cheek and embraced me with such affection that I must have passed. Camilla then performed her 'inspection,' and I passed once more.

"You look amazing, Jon!" she exclaimed, kissing me on the cheek. I swear she'd grown two inches when I last saw Diana three months ago. The prom began at 7:30 p.m. at a nearby restaurant on Long Island Sound, right on the beach. I left at 6:30 a.m. to pick up Diana, waiting along the way for her parents to take photographs of us. I sat with her father Harold, Walt, and Will, chatting as the twins smiled at me with smart-ass grins. They were aware of information that I was unaware of.

When Diana came downstairs ten minutes later, I figured out what it was. She was dressed in a light pink satin robe with spaghetti straps that clung to her frame. She also wore a similar pair of satin high-heeled sandals. Her hair was styled about her head, with a few wisps loose around her face. Her mother loaned her a collection of pearls, a choker, which enhanced the elegance of her neck. Diana looked like a goddess to me after some light lipstick. I could see why her brothers were laughing now. They expected me to be swept off my feet.

"You're...a glimpse of loveliness," I said, kissing Diana's cheek to avoid ruining her lipstick.

She sent me a nervous smile, but she managed to say, "Thank you so much, Jon. I'm feeling really pretty."

"Pretty doesn't even begin to describe it. You're gorgeous, honey." I kissed her once more. Then I offered her a wrist corsage and assisted her in putting it on.

"Thank you, sweetheart," Diana said as she gently kissed my face. I caught a scent of her scent, something light, and expensive smelling, and I felt I was going to die of joy.

Her parents snapped photos, and even the twins were in on the action. They stood to either side of their far smaller sibling, brushing her cheeks and surprising her—photos of her with her parents, both individually and together. And, of course, a swarm with me, hugging each other closer than we might have wanted. But we did take one shot where we held each other tightly and looked into each other's eyes. It was a staged picture, but there was nothing phony about how we looked when taking it. We were madly in lust, and it was obvious. She brought a tiny pack, which I accepted, and we said our final goodbyes to her dad.

We then had to return to my house to take more photos for my dad. This time, we had to share a huge kiss with Camilla, my parents, and other members of our family. We couldn't help ourselves. When we got in my vehicle, I assisted Diana in getting back in as my neighbors stood outside and smiled at us. It was somewhat embarrassing, but these were people I had met for the majority of my life. It was very touching. We stowed her cashmere wrap in the back seat, and I drove to our wedding.

Diana said as she walked around the block, "Take a look at Jon. I can't save myself from kissing you!" Never one to turn down a girl, I found a spot to pull over, and we locked into a massive embrace, complete with a slew of loving kisses.

"Honey, I adore you. And I can't get over how stunning you are. You're going to outperform all the other kids!"

"I'm not sure about that. I know I'll be escorted by the most attractive man in the room. Like the character in the Marlboro commercials. Beautiful and tough!"

"I'm not sure about that," I replied in her terms, but I was ecstatic that she felt I was even remotely attractive. I wasn't, but I was in her eyes.

"Yes, I do. Jon, you're stunning. To me, that is. That is all that is essential." She was right. We kissed again, took a few minutes to let Diana patch her lipstick, and then we were on our way.

Our class rented a restaurant right on Long Island Sound, near the Throgs Neck Bridge. It was still light outside when it began, but when it became darker and the bridge, ships, and houses along the water lit up, the view became as romantic as it could be. We had a great time listening to quick and slow music together. I liked keeping Diana in front of everybody during those slow songs. Not that she was the most stunning person there (though she was), just so that we could show everybody how deeply we cared about each other. Some partners may have liked each other, but I couldn't picture it being anything like what we did about each other if I'm biased.

A delicious seafood meal was prepared, a couple of flasks were discreetly passed around (I declined; I don't drink and drive), and we joked and spoke with friends and colleagues while having a wonderful time. We went outside with a few other couples before dessert and just loved being there, staring out at the lake and the largely blue sky. I wrapped Diana's wrap around her neck because it was comfortable by the lake.

"Thank you so much, sweetheart. You still show me affection. I'm completely smitten with you."

"It's not difficult to fall in love with you. You have such a beautiful heart." She grinned when I kissed her on the face.

"Do we plan on heading to the beach after the party?"

"That's the overall strategy." After prom, it was customary to go to Jones Beach, a massive beach complex on Nassau County's south shore, make a large fire, and then... At least, it was the custom.

"Do you mind if we skipped the pool party? My parents do not want me to return before noon. They are, as I previously said, very understanding."

"I'd be able to hang out until late in the morning. My parents are aware that we are...intimate. They are aware that this is a rare event. I have a change of clothes with me, and I'm sure you do as well. But where do we go from here?"

"I assumed we'd go to a hotel and spend the night together. If you so like." Diana seemed unsure, as though I would say no to her.

"If I so desire? You can bet you pretty little tush that I do. I'd like to spend the night alone with you, sleep with you, and then make love to you in the morning. Things we haven't been able to achieve in the past. I don't want to share you with someone tonight. Are you certain you want to?"

"Jon, I've been worrying about it all day. In reality, we should sneak out right now..."

Then we made our choice. We said our goodbyes to a few individuals, mainly old friends of mine, and left about an hour before the party started. We went to a nearby Holiday Inn, which is often safe and reasonably priced, and I booked us to space with a 9 a.m. wake-up call. I got our bags, and we went to our space on the third level, oblivious to the fact that other visitors in the lobby and even the elDianator were staring at us. We broke out laughing, embracing, and hugging when we got to our bed. That was the type of feeling it was.

We soon quit laughing; we desperately missed each other, and this was our first opportunity to take our time with each other and spend an entire night together. We immediately hugged each other and kissed with hungry lust. We didn't say much at first, only kissed as she helped me take off my scarf, then my bow tie. "Is that a true bow tie? What if you don't have a clip-on? I'm blown away!" Diana laughed softly, sexily.

"My mother had to tie it for me," I said into her ear as I kissed the side of her cheek.

"Do you mind doing me a favor, sweetheart? And don't bring up your mother when we're doing this." We chuckled again, and I vowed not to bring up my mother for a bit. Diana moaned as I kissed the side of her throat, her beautiful neck with choker pearls at the base. She cocked her head to the side to allow me more entry, and I avoided the urge to bite her there, but I wasn't interested in leaving hickeys. I kissed her down to her back, taking the spaghetti strap of her gown down. "Jon, that's fantastic," Diana said as she cradled my cheek. "Don't forget to do the other line." I kissed across her chest, pulled down the other strap, and kissed her shoulder again, as I had done on the other line. I reached behind her and steadily pulled down the back zipper, allowing us to hear each collection of teeth release. The tone was very enticing.

I eventually made it to the bottom, and we let her gown slip down her body, softly floating onto the floor with a gentle satin tone. Diana drew the nude-colored cups over her breasts, which was another impressive sight for me. She was now only wearing a pair of nude and lacy string briefs, a pair of nude thigh-high stockings, and her light pink sandals. Delectable. "Diana, you're stunning. The most beautiful lady I've ever seen anywhere." My gaze was drawn to her.

"You're such a sweetie, kid. You make me feel like the most stunning woman on the planet."

"As far as I'm concerned, you are. To me, you'll always be the most beautiful lady." Diana prevented me from unbuttoning my sweater.

"That's my responsibility, sweetheart." She kissed my neck as she undid my buttons, licking my chest with each one. Through her lips on my body, she led the way. I closed my eyes and focused solely on the sensations, particularly when her tongue snuck out and took a brief taste of my body.

I ran my fingertips through her silky hair and down her back, causing her to shiver and gasp as she continued down my body. Diana threw my top aside and opened my jeans, pulling my zipper down in the same calculated slow motion she used to open my shirt. We continued kissing down, and when the zipper was almost down, Diana reached down and flitted her fingertips over the bulge of my cock in my underwear. That made me whine, and I was itching to get out of my jeans. As Diana helped me get my pants off, I kicked off my heels, leaving us both in our underwear. Our embraces and gestures were more intense when we wear fewer. Lust and passion are a powerful mix, and we were engrossed in both.

I took my little love to the bed and softly lay her back. "Be right back in five seconds," I said as I turned on a tiny lamp and turned off the main room lights. The lamp was far enough away from the bed to offer us a glow to enable us to see each other without being too light.

"Take off your underwear before you get in bed with me," Diana said, rubbing her pantyhose. I stood a few steps away from the bed and bent down to slip my underwear down my thighs, staring at her. Diana raised her hips and pulled her panties off, revealing only her stockings and sandals. "Stay there, sweetheart. I'll play with your cunt if you stroke my dick." She pulled her knees apart, allowing me to have a good look at her lovely cunt.

My cock had been hard for a long time before that, and having her splayed for me made my dick hop up and down without touching it. "Take a look at what you're doing to me, sexy lady." I jumped a few more times.

"I like how you do it. It has an impact on me that I can't quite put my finger on. To mention, you turn me on like no other guy I've ever fantasized about." Her fingertips were circling her mouth, so I grabbed my cock and stroked it. I'd never considered jerking off in front of a woman before, but doing so with the love of my life as she revealed herself to me was unbelievably sexy. As I jerked off painfully, my feet were separated, and my legs were slightly bent, and Diana inserted two fingers into her gaping cunt. When she rubbed her clit with her other hand's finger, her hips rose off the bed. Her palm was gleaming with her fluids, which were also running down her thighs and butt. I had to slow it down because the sight was so sexy that I might have passed out without ever holding her.

"I need you right now, honey. I need both your body and your core. I can hardly wait, "I was desperate, I said.

"Come on in, sweetheart. Don't put that off any longer." She felt about as desperate as I did. I walked swiftly, jumped onto the bunk, and was inside her in a matter of seconds. Her thighs were around my ass, smoother than average in the pricey stockings, as we fucked each other with impunity. We might make love later. However, we had immediate needs to respond to. We were still so pumped up that it didn't take long, maybe a dozen or so thrusts before Diana appeared, scratching at my back as she gasped. After a half-dozen more, it was my turn, gripping her

237

butt with as hard a grip as I could and grunting from deep inside my mouth. Until my lips met hers, she kissed my neck and stomach.

"Diana, I adore you. A day, every day, every day, every day, every day, every day, every day, every day, every" I kissed her again, this time in deep breaths.

"And I adore you as well, sweetheart. Outstanding individual. "She teased my cheek and neck with her fingertips. Her contact was exceptional.

The low illumination of the lamp provided enough illumination for us to see in the space as we lay there. We were lying on our sides, palms clasped. I needed to pee after a bit, so I asked Diana if she wanted to go first. "Thank you for being so chivalrous," she smiled. "But you have the choice of going first. I'll gather a couple of items, and then it'll be my time. So go ahead and do it, boy. I'm excited to spend the evening with you. And don't imagine for a second that we're finished for the night. More fun is on the way."

I kissed her again before entering the bathroom and doing what I needed to do. I peed, cleaned up a little, brushed and flossed my teeth. I lost my socks, so I came out nude, and Diana gave me a standing ovation. "Ballbuster," I grunted, then lightly spanked her as I passed past.

"You'll be sorry when you see what I'm carrying to bed. After all, I could not let you near me, "As she ducked into the toilet, she said with a grin.

I knew she'd take a while, so I pulled out the nice hanger I'd taken with me and hung up my tux and coat, wrapping the bowtie around the rack and hanging it in the wardrobe, where Diana had hung up her gown. We were also kind people, which boded well for our future if one existed.

When I finished everything I wanted to do, I climbed back into bed and waited for Diana. Diana was well worth the wait for the second time that night. Her hair was down below her shoulders, and she was dressed in a black satin nightgown that reached down to her upper thighs and had lace detailing along the sides except for the armholes. But the neckline and hem were pure black lace, and she appeared incredibly seductive. The principle of fewer is more strongly applicable.

"That's incredible. You never cease to amaze me. "I said this with genuine respect and desire. "Are you certain you're just 18? You seduce me as though you're far older!"

"I know what I want and what I want. I bought this little number at a lingerie shop the other day. I can see you're impressed. "Diana said this as she bent one knee and rubbed her hand up and down her chest, from thigh to breast. She was an expert at playing the role of a seductress.

"Impressed isn't quite close to describing how I'm feeling. My darling, please go to bed. Let's see what I believe."

Diana turned off the light. The space was dim, but there was plenty of light streaming in through the thin white curtains that ran along with the doors. We had thicker curtains for when we went to bed, but that was later. The light in the space created a romantic mood.

Diana crawled in with me as I pulled up the blanket and top sheet. Diana said this as she snuggled up to me, her petite body fitting too well in my bigger frame. "This is indeed a first for me. Have you ever stayed up all night with a girl?"

"Never, ever. It's also a first for me. Diana, you're not a child. You are fully feminine. A stunning, lustful, sexy, brilliant, and amusing lady. Is there something I've forgotten?" As I kissed her soft lips, I said.

"Just one thing. I'm in love. My gorgeous man, I adore you. My hottie." We kissed like long-distance lovers, passionate, hungry, and a little crazy about each other. We made out like that in bed, rolling across the bed with each other, but gently. We were intensely passionate, but we were taking our time. That night, we had enough of it.

The satin of her nightgown felt cool and slippery against my skin, which was a massive turn on in and of itself. But it wasn't as much of a turn-on as the lady wearing it. Diana's insides were still scorching, and her nipples created hard little bumps through the sexy material. As we continued kissing, I ran my fingertips over those thick nubs, and she rubbed her palms over my bald, hairy chest. We were both moanings, eager for more with my hard cock running down her inner thigh, but we both realized that the longer we waited, the more painful our encounter would get. Then we told ourselves to wait, touching and teasing but still waiting. As our excitement grew, I kissed the side of Diana's neck and down along her back, and she closed her eyes and gasped.

"Jon, you are making me insane! More than a bit, fuck! Take me right away! My sexy guy, I need you!"

"My love, whatever you like! My sexy queen, I'm more than happy for you!" I picked her and yanked her up to the roof. I snagged her negligee just enough to assist her in mounting me. She raised her butt just enough to position the head of my cock against her pussy, and her eyes widened when my cock slipped smoothly and easily into her pussy. Diana then closed her eyes for a moment as she arched her back and rubbed her hands through her hair and across her tits. I couldn't say anything because she was so beautiful and sensual. I was taken aback by her beauty and eroticism. She bit her lower lip while her legs swung up and down, my cock buried deep inside her.

"Honey, if you could see yourself right now, you'd see what I see... the most enticing sight in the universe!" I said as my hands caressed her thighs and then moved up her body, both over and under her nightgown.

"Tell me what you see," Diana asked, her voice trembling. "Say it to me, girl."

"Your face is breathtaking, and your body moves like it's in a party. I hope this moment will last forever. I'm madly in love with you. I am ecstatic about you."

Diana grinned as she opened her eyes, already trapped in her pleasures. "My handsome friend, you pull it out of me. My honey, you're a total babe. She shifted slowly and steadily in what was perhaps the most incredible sex we'd ever experienced. Our previous mad fuck was making things easier to avoid rushing this time. Diana had a couple of soft orgasms, which I induced by pressing her clitoris with my thumb.

"God, I love it when you do that to me!" she exclaimed after the second climax. "I don't care who taught you that, but I do want to thank her." Diana continued to ground her ass into my body, and my cock was stirring up her juices. As our bodies were locked together, I reached for her hands, and we locked fingers. We looked each other in the eyes and rode the waves of joy we experienced.

"I'm not going to say anybody, honey. All that counts is how much fun we're having with each other."

"There's no argument here," Diana said as her body prepared to cum again. I was prepared as well, so I flipped her on her back and pushed more forcefully to strengthen both of our orgasms. She drew her legs back and drew down the left side of her nightgown, revealing her breast. "Suck me, sexy one," says the sexy man. I couldn't, and I didn't want to. My tongue reached her nipple and sucked it as deep as it would go into my mouth. Diana kept crying, "I love this, I love you."

"I adore you as well, my lovely lady. A great deal. "As I grew closer to cumming, I grunted. It reached me a minute later, and I plunged deep inside Diana, holding my hips there, twitching as I ejaculated thick jets of my cum. The sensation of being filled triggered Diana, and she dug her fingernails into my biceps as she joined me in her intense climax. I landed on her, taking the majority of my weight off her, and kissed her down her neck and up to her lips. "Honey, I adore you. Almost always."

"I adore you as well, sweetheart." Diana was smiling up at me, and the sight of caring on her face was palpable. I shifted to her hand, and we clutched each other as though our futures relied on it. There was no doubt in my head that our romantic life was the strongest it could ever be, and we were in love with each other.

We nuzzled each other, giggling, playing, and enjoying each other. We could both see why couples enjoy sleeping together. It could be a lot of fun, particularly if it were something you had never done before.

We took turns using the toilet for a bit, and then we settled in to sleep together—actually SLEEP together. They were in the same room as the majority of partners. Diana snuggled into my lap, like she had done many times before, except this time was different. This was special.

"Jon, thank you for a fantastic evening. I had a fantastic time. But for our first date, this was perhaps the greatest evening I've ever had. That was also incredible. I can't make up my mind. "Diana was on the brink of falling asleep.

I kissed her on the cheek and whispered, "I thought it was fantastic as well. Then there's always the morning. Maybe we should have a shower together." She just made a contented sound as she fell asleep with my arm around her. I wondered if I should sleep like that, but I didn't think about it too long. I could have dozed off a couple of minutes later.

XXXXXXXXXXXXXXXXXXXXXXXXXXXXXXXXXXXXXXXXXX
XXXXXXXXXXXXXXXXXXXXXXXXXXXXXXXXXXXXXXXXXX
XXXXXXXXXXXXXXXXXX

The alarm went off at 9 a.m., and we sat up painfully in bed. Diana wasn't on top of me now, but she wasn't far from in the queen size tent. She rolled towards me, and despite her tired skin, unbrushed hair, and lack of lipstick, she was beautiful, just lovely. Her grin alone made my heart skip a beat. "Good day, my Queen. Did you have a good night's sleep?" I questioned her politely.

"Is she your Queen? Just if you happen to be my King. And, yeah, I slept well. You just wore me out there."

"I'm afraid I can't be your King. I'd rather serve you as a farmer. For instance, under your benign reign." We were giggling as a result of the hilarity.

"Did you mean to say "serve me" or "service me"? Since I just enjoy being served by you, my King."

"Servant," I said emphatically. "It's my game, and I make the rules."

"Well, well, if you want," Diana said as if I had to impose it on her. In practice, she was wide-eyed, dreaming about her part in my little dream.

"Next time, I'll be the King, and you can be my serving wench," I said, giggling.

"MMMMM, or maybe I should just be my King's toy. There are too many more! But for the time being,' Diana said as she stepped out of her niqab, "You must see to the needs of your Queen. When I've used the restroom!" She dashed for the toilet, her tiny breasts jiggling beautifully, making me wait my turn. I was hard from the morning wood (a piss hardon) and from anticipating our kinky pleasure. But first, I had to clear my bladder. I knew I was about to explode.

"Diana, darling, are you finished in there?" I knocked. I inquired, a little pleadingly.

"In a matter of minutes! I need to clean my teeth and do a few other things!"

I was moving in there as soon as she was through with the bathroom. Diana gasped when I opened the door and dashed for the bowl. "What are you doing, Jon? Are you gone insane? Get the hell back!"

"I can't do it; I need to pee urgently!" I stood there and peed in front of Diana, who was standing a few steps away at the sink, in front of the mirror, dumbfounded. As happiness washed through me, I let out a deep sigh. When Diana stared at me, I forced my cock downwards to get my pee in the bowl where it belonged. Not at me, but at my dick, which eventually relaxed as the pain from my bladder subsided and my erection disappeared. When we got to it, I wasn't concerned; we'd get it up to full workforce in seconds. But before it became limp, Diana reached over and softly took my cock in her right hand as pee continued to run through my pipe. When she watched the stream flow by, I was taken aback. I went full-on hard in seconds, just as I finished relieving myself. I had to use a stiffy to shake off the remaining fall.

"Diana? Are you going to let go of my cock sometime soon?" She seemed to be trapped in some kind of sexual modern universe and didn't appear to notice me entirely.

"Huh? No, well... not yet. Come here." I flushed the toilet and shuffled next to her, her arms still lovingly gripping me. She ran the water in the sink and soaped her hand before washing my cock with tender loving attention, kneeling in front of me. When she was doing that, I bent over and washed my hands. This was a bit strange and very humid. She stood up and dragged my cock across the drain, vigorously rinsing it out, "There. All set to make your Queen happy," she said, standing on her toes and kissing me with passion and playfulness.

"Let me just clean my teeth, my love, and stay right here," I said as Diana stood nearby, twisting back and forth like a tiny sex kitten, a little giggle escaping her lips.

"You've got me so hot, girl," she said before licking my lip. I almost spat out my toothpaste when I was done, but I kept my cool and rinsed my mouth while the tip of her tongue stuck in my ear. I wiped my brow and turned to pick Diana up beneath her arms and knees as though she weighed nothing. I sat on the bed with my Queen, bending over her and kissing her warmly. She stroked my cheek and said, "You're all rough, like sandpaper. It's very masculine, very sexy. Normally your Queen will order you to shave before approaching Us, but We'll forgive you this time, knave," and it was nice and amusing, and it was sexy as hell.

"Now, knave, serve your Queen, and eat the royal cunt!"

I almost couldn't get something done because I laughed too hard, but I pulled myself together enough to get back into the groove of things. "As you wish, m'lady; I am here to please my Queen," I said, nestling my head between her legs and licking her swollen lips. As I probed and examined Diana's sweet gash, I rubbed my face back and forth, gripping onto her thighs. She shuddered, then tensed when I reached her most vulnerable spots, and she screamed as her legs flailed around my head. "Am I pleasing you, my Queen? Am I serving you well?" I asked, laughing slightly.

"All right, my knave. Outstandingly well. But don't stop servicing Us," my Queen said as she climbed the ladder into her climax. I went back at her, sucking on her lips, sucking her whole pussy as I swirled around her clit. A minute more of that, and her body shook all over, and I let her clit bounce on the tip of my tongue.

"Can I kiss the sweet lips of my Queen?" "

"Of course, you're right, knave. We would be a negligent Queen if we ignored my knave after doing such a wonderful job."

"Um, my Queen, you are aware that the word 'knave' refers to an unscrupulous individual."

Diana, my Queen, stared at me as though she had gone insane: "It is not! "

"Yes, my genius, it is. "I promise you that."

"Fuck! " Throughout our game, I kept calling you that! I apologize! I'll transform you into a Knight! Mr. Sexy Guy! "

"I believe your Majesty has restrictions on who she might call a knight after Magna Carta," we were having fun with this.

"Well, I dunno how I'm going to make amends to my sorry serf." The Queen's service! "

I was all set to let Diana work her magic on me when I saw the time: 10:20, and we had to check out at 11! "No time, my Queen! We're going to be late! I'll shave and resume the shower right away! You pack as many as you can, and I'll get the remainder. We'll wash together, and there will be NO nonsense. We have 40 minutes to find out! " We were frantic, running around to get everything packed, taking a quick shower together, grooming as best we could, dressing, and gathering the previous night's things. We were online to check out at the front desk at 11, but we were safe. Otherwise, I might have been stuck for an extra half-day. Not the end of the world, so why pay it if it's unnecessary?

"OK, honey, what's the matter?" Please let me."

"You did such a great job servicing your 'Queen,' and I didn't do much for you other than turn you all on." I'm sorry, sweetheart."

"Please don't be sorry. This morning was fantastic. You'll make amends with me over the week. Maybe tomorrow. You're not supposed to be mad when I'm not."

"You're the only boyfriend anyone might ask for." Thank you so much, Jon, my darling. I swear I'll make it up to you." We sat and had a huge meal, then I dropped her off at home right before noon and returned shortly after. My parents were cool, and Camilla didn't tease me or smash balls; I guess she knew enough not to make a big deal of it.

Because of the prom, there was no homework that weekend, but there was learning, and that's what I was doing when my phone rang at 4 p.m., and I said, "Hello, my beautiful Queen."

Adrienne's voice came over the phone line next: "I think that was for Diana?" Hello, Jon. How are you? "

"Uh, Ade, I'm fine; I called you a few times, but you didn't respond or return my calls."

I know. I couldn't speak to you, Jon. I was too angry. And I'm sorry. I wasn't upset because of that dumb towel. Well, maybe a little. I was upset because...I was convinced you and Diana were a permanent thing, and it wouldn't improve. I was foolish. I'm so sorry. Jon."

"You don't need to apologize, Ade. I understood that you were mad, and it's all forgiven now. I always love you."

"Jon, could you still be my escort Friday night? I know it's sort of last minute, but I don't have anyone else to go with." She seemed lonely, and I wanted to support her. But it wasn't just my choice.

"Ade, I have to call you back in five minutes, okay? Talk to you in a moment," I said as I dialed Diana's number. It was as much her choice as it was mine.

I came to the stage after we exchanged hellos, and I love yous. "Honey, Adrienne called me and asked if I would still take her to her prom. To make a long story short, she asked if I would still take her to her prom. I told her I needed to chat about it with you first. I remember you said it was fine with you a couple of weeks back, so I wanted to make sure you still feel that way. If you don't, then that's it."

"Jon, you can't blame anything on me. If I want to say no, I don't want you to take her, so you and Adrienne would be over as friends. She'll be hurt, and she'll blame that on me. You've said she was your best friend before I came along. I can't take anyone that important from you. In the long run, it will hurt you too, and I don't want to do that that would hurt you.

"And I assure you, Adrienne and I are going as friends only," I said as I hung up the phone so I could call Ade back. I informed her I'd be happy to accompany her, and I could hear her grin over the cell.

"Thank you from the bottom of my heart, Jon, and please thank Diana for me; I can't believe this is simple for her."

"She's fine with it, Ade. She wants to be your buddy because she understands how precious you are to me, and you'll always be special to me, whatever happens with Diana and me, I swear."

"Me too. So, Friday night, ok? Be at my house by 7? We'll do some videos, and then the prom begins at 7:30. And Jon?"

"It's my pleasure, Ade, and I'll see you on Friday."

Diana and I ran into each other a couple of times in the week. We made love once; then, she offered me a spectacular blowjob in my car as retaliation for Saturday morning. She didn't hurry it; instead of dragging things out, taking me to the verge of cumming and cooling me off a couple of times before bringing me to a howling orgasm. I can't talk to the other men, but she was familiar with my body. That was more than sufficient for me.

Diana and I spent an hour after school Friday, both kissing and cuddling in my car until I had to pick up my tux (Milton offered me a break this time; it was the same tux) and prepare to head up to Westchester. Not because of Adrienne, but because Friday night was our date night, she was a little sad when we had to say goodbye. Every Friday night, we went out. On Saturdays, we occasionally went out, and on some, we stayed in and relaxed, but Friday was still date night. "Call me when you get up tomorrow? I realize you'll be home late today. Honestly, if her parents ask if you want to hang over instead of driving an hour home late at night, do it. I'd feel happier if you did. Not that I'll know. Just be careful, sweetheart. I love you."

Diana grinned, a little sad when I kissed her lip. "Thank you, honey. I'll stay if they inquire, then we'll make up for tonight tomorrow. We'll do something casual and something Very fun!" I said as I kissed her passionately.

"Don't bet on it; I should be having my period any day now, probably tomorrow or Sunday, so I will keep my sexy man proud," she said as she squeezed my dick.

"As tempting as that is, if you have to forego it, so do I; there are plenty of other ways for us to have fun without sex."

"We'll deal with it tomorrow; now get out of here before I pull you into my house and lock you up."
"Oh, that might be interesting! We'll have to do that sometime!"
We smiled, kissed, and said our good-nights. I returned home, a little disappointed, picked up the tux, showered, shaved, and was on my way. Marvin and Sandy, who were like second parents to me, greeted me at the door and entertained me as we waited for Adrienne. They promised to let me sleepover, which I gratefully embraced, and they called my parents to notify them, which I'm sure was a comfort for them as well. Then Adrienne arrived, and she looked fantastic, just as good as Diana had the

week before. Her gown was made of black chiffon and layered over a black shell. Her hair was curled in a nice wave that floated across her shoulders. If I were a less devoted kind of guy...

"Ade, you look beautiful!" I kissed her face, and she grinned at me, her bright red lipstick matching her almost milk-white face.

"Thank you, Jon. You look very handsome yourself." She gently grabbed my hand and added, "Thank you for doing this. I appreciate it. And make sure you thank Diana." We took photographs (it's a routine) and went to the country club where the prom was held.

Ade's prom was more extravagant than mine; she lived in a wealthy neighborhood where the families were well-off, and it showed. It was in a country club's banquet area, with very good decorations and fantastic cuisine, a seven-piece band...you get the picture. We gathered at a table of her best colleagues, all of whom were there on dates rather than escorts. I tried my hardest to make her feel unique by dancing next to her during the slow songs, but I only kissed her on the cheek a couple of times. I didn't want to push her. It was a wonderful evening...and I missed Diana in an almost excruciating way. My heart was complete with her, and I felt I had made a mistake by accompanying my mate.

After the party, we were asked to attend a big group at an after-party at one of the guys' places. Adrienne tried to go, but I had the feeling it was going to be a make-out session (and a lot more), something I couldn't do. No way, not with her. As I told her I didn't want to do it, Adrienne exclaimed, "Why the heck not, Jon? It's just some kissing and things."

"Ade, why not? I'm in love with Diana, and I'm not cheating on her; you realized that before making the arrangements. Besides, you know there's going to be a lot of hooking up there; that can't happen."

"Wow, for Christ's sake, what's your problem? Am I so repulsive to you? Don't you find me attractive? I know how I look in this gown; you might virtually rip it off me tonight and do anything you want. I'll never say. Diana won't know."

"I See. I won't do it to her. I can't, Adrienne. If I asked you for guidance on another girl as a friend, what would you say? Would you encourage me to do that, to cheat on Diana?" I was irritated with her, and it showed.

"It's not any other person. It's me, we're as tight as friends can be, and dammit, I want you tonight. I've wanted you for a long time. Please, Jon. Don't make me beg." Tears welled up in her eyes, and I felt terrible for all of us. I was letting her down, and it was hurting her. Yet I couldn't do what she demanded of me.

"Ade," you say.

"Don't tell me that!" she nearly yelled at me. Some citizens were now looking at us. This was getting out of hand. "Stop acting as you worry for me!"

"I love you a lot, so I'm not going to sleep with you. Let's go; I'd better take you home," I said as she yanked my hand away.

"Don't worry! I'll get another lift from a true pal!" That hurt a lot because I was just as frustrated as she was. Yet, I kept my cool. I didn't want to suggest anything I'd regret later.

"Adrienne, are you sure? I don't like the thought of having you here like this." Karen, a friend of hers, came over and said, "I'll make sure she gets home all right. Just go, Jon. You've hurt her enough." I was feeling foolish.

"Fine. When you're able to speak rationally, you know my phone," I said sternly as I walked away on my own. I was enraged as I got to my vehicle. I was upset and hurt because I was trying to be a good person to uphold my commitment to my girlfriend.

It was after 11 p.m., and I wanted to see Diana so that I wouldn't be able to until at least midnight. I was embarrassed to call her at that hour, but I wanted to speak with her. I pulled into a gas station and used the payphone to dial Diana's house while the attendant refueled my vehicle. Her father answered the phone, not thrilled to be answering the phone at 11:15 a.m., but he could see I sounded irritated, so he dialed Diana's extension.

"What's up, Jon? Are you okay?"

"I am NOT ok. This has been a horrible evening. I'll be back in Queens in about an hour. May I come over and chat? No funny business, I just want to talk."

"Ok, come on over; I'll be ready. We'll go for coffee and talk; just drive carefully, sweetheart. I love you."

"I love you, honey; I'll be careful; I'll see you in about an hour."

I rode slowly, as promised, and arrived at Diana's house in less than an hour. As soon as she saw me drive up, she came down her road and got in the vehicle. I hugged her in my embrace and kissed her passionately before pulling away. And I burst into tears. I had no option.

Diana just kissed me and let me weep, not rushing me to get in the car, even though we were right in front of her house and several lights were turned on. After a few minutes, she asked if I needed her to drive, and I informed her I'd be grateful if she could. So I got out and circled my vehicle, and she slid over and drove my car for the first time. She had to pull the bench seat all the way forward to hit the brakes, which made me laugh, which made me feel stronger. We went to the neighborhood diner and were placed at a tiny table. We ordered decaf coffee and dessert, and I told her how what began off as a pleasant evening turned into a catastrophe.

Diana found it difficult to relate to the plot. Telling her effectively stopped the possibility of her and Adrienne being mates. It also said that my relationship with Adrienne was almost done. It would be too much to expect Diana to forget what Adrienne wanted to convince me to do, which was to cheat on Diana. The idea that I had lost Ade as a friend for good was destroying me. If Diana and I split up, I'd be missing any of them. I was furious at Ade for bringing me into that situation.

We had finished our coffee and pie by the time I finished the novel. We remained quiet for a moment as Diana mulled about the tale in her mind. "I'm sorry this hurt you so badly, sweetheart; I'm sorry she placed you in that position, but I'm so glad my boyfriend is so trustworthy; I trusted you tonight, and I'll still trust you." Diana inquired.

"If anything, I understated it. She looked beautiful. And as we danced, all I could think of was how much I missed you. I love Adrienne as a companion, nothing else. I worry about her. I'm going to lose her now. But missing you will be a thousand times worse." I softly grasped her back. "Maybe a million times worse. I'm madly in love with you, and if we weren't so young..."

"What if we weren't so young, Jon?"

"I guess I'd invite you to marry me. Isn't that ridiculous?"

"I don't think so; in reality, I would say yes."

We were staring at each other as though we couldn't believe what we were doing. As if we were insane. Then we looked into it. Diana wore casual denim and a long-sleeve patterned sweater while I wore a tuxedo. We weren't close to being incongruous. We didn't know what to think next.

Diana said something. "Jon, take me somewhere and make love to me. Our parking spot, the football field, anywhere, wherever."

I paid the bill, then we got in my car and drove to our little parking spot. There was another car there, but there was plenty of room for me. I got my blanket (which was constantly washed), and we spread out as best we could in the backseat. We cuddled so tightly that it was as though we had all the room in the universe.

Our mouths were always in contact, alternating little kisses with large ones, softly and tightly rubbing, needing each other. We took Diana's jeans and underwear off, then my pants, but she insisted on keeping my ruffled top on. "You look so damn good in that tee," she chuckled lustfully.

"You look sexy in something," I retorted. "Or, sometimes, none at all." As the head of my hard dick moved through her pubic hair, I kissed her.

"Thank you so much. You have a way of making a girl feel sexy. "As she drew my head to her left breast, she said. "Suck my breast, please. That makes me so happy, my love." My cock made its way to the entrance to her vagina while her thighs were spread apart. We were locked together, blissfully united as waves of affection and desire poured through us, with a simple thrust forward. I pushed my arms under Diana's elbows, pulling her legs farther back, allowing me a perfect position to offer her the most satisfaction. With each stroke, my cock rubbed over her clit, and she shuddered. We continued kissing instead of chatting, then I returned to suck one of her nipples, and Diana emerged from the extra scrutiny. Her hips wiggled underneath me, causing strong vibrations in my cock through my glans. Her gestures prompted me to ramp up my own, and we were quickly on the verge of a mind-boggling climax.

She was the first to arrive; her past orgasms had held her on the verge of the greatest one. "Jon, hurry up. I'm doing my best to wait for you, my darling. Don't keep me waiting for long."

"Almost my love," I murmured, and with a couple more strokes, I was there with her. I grunted, arched my back, and we had an amazing, loving orgasm that numbed both of our senses. We scarcely moved as we hugged each other, exchanging our warmth and affection.

I remained inside Diana until my cock faded and dropped out, leaking some of our shared fluids into the blanket. We kept touching each other, enjoying the physical and emotional interaction. It was just past two o'clock. I had taken the next day off from college, as I had the week prior. It was a good job I did because there was no chance I might have gone to work the next (same) day. My bosses were understanding; prom season arrives just once in a lifetime.

We changed our clothes and stayed there for a bit, cuddled and cozy. However, there was a large goose egg in the air surrounding us.

I was the first to talk. "Honey, were we serious when I asked if I should propose to you, and you said you would say yes? If only we weren't so young."

"I believe we were at the time. I've considered it...or maybe fantasized about it. I'm madly in love with you as well. It will have to be a LONG commitment. "She laughed.

"Yes, it has been years. I believe our parents will have a stroke. There were just four of them."

We stood there, palms clasped. We understood we had to go, but we were dreading it. "There's something else we need to discuss, Jon. A more pressing problem. My camp agreement is already on my desk. Would I be moving there this summer? Are you certain you couldn't come work with me there? I'm not sure how we'll manage being separated all summer, except on my one day off each week. I'm going to be lonely without you, baby." I saw a woman cry for the second time that night as a result of me. I was physically spent. Yet I couldn't abandon her.

"I'm afraid I can't, honey. It seems to be a fantastic place to spend the summer. But I promised that would provide me with the majority of the funds I need for the year. Diana, I don't have a couple hundred thousand dollars waiting for me. I don't want to press my parents for more funds that they still provide to help compensate for education and other necessities."

"How about I help you make up the gap between what you'll receive at camp and what you'll earn at the print shop?"

I stared at her as if she were crazy. "No way, no how. Diana, I'm not taking your income. I couldn't do it."

"But would you make me pay for a hotel room or when we go out to eat once in a while? What's the distinction?" She inquired, evidently distressed. It wasn't easy to understand what was different, but it was important for me.

"Honey, it's been a busy day and a difficult evening. Will we discuss this tomorrow? I guarantee it. You can come to my house, or I can come to you, whichever is more convenient for you. Please offer me until 1 p.m. Will you please?" I was genuinely pleading with her because I was so tired.

"Fine, we'll work it out tomorrow, Jon." Diana's eyes were filled with passion, despite her attempts to appear cold.

We kept hands as I walked, and we arrived at her house in ten minutes. We exchanged goodnight kisses and hugs in my seat, and when she went to get out, I moved to walk her to the door as normal. "Don't do that, sweetheart. I can see it in your eyes that you're tired. Only keep an eye on me before I move into my building. Jon, I adore you. When you wake up tomorrow, please call me. I'll be alert."

"Honey, I'm too tired to disagree with you. I adore you as well. I'll contact you, and we'll work things out. Good night, everybody." I stood there watching until she got to the entrance, grinned at me, and went inside. I dragged myself home, which was luckily just five minutes from. I was half asleep when I opened the front door, but before I went to sleep, I knocked on my parents' door to let them know I was home; they had expected me to spend the night at Adrienne's parents' place. I told them I'd call them in the morning, went to my place, changed out of my tux, and climbed into bed naked. I couldn't really clean my teeth or bathe. That's how exhausted I was. I fell asleep in seconds and slept until 11 a.m.

Lightning Source UK Ltd.
Milton Keynes UK
UKHW021424310521
384684UK00002B/561

9 781803 014043